MW01087552

The Rela~~tionship is the Project~~

JADE LILLIE (she/her) is a facilitator and specialist in community and stakeholder engagement. She has worked throughout Australia and South-East Asia in strategy, advocacy, program design, community-engaged practice and industry development. She conceived *The Relationship is the Project* following her role as Director and CEO at Footscray Community Arts and as a Sidney Myer Creative Fellow.

KATE LARSEN (she/her) is a writer, arts and cultural consultant with more than 25 years experience in the non-profit, government and cultural sectors in Australia, Asia and the UK. She is a thought leader in the areas of arts governance and cultural leadership, workplace culture and wellbeing, online communication and communities, and inclusion and community leadership of under-represented groups.

CARA KIRKWOOD (she/her) is a national advocate and influencer for Aboriginal and Torres Strait Islander people, art, culture and creative industries. Currently the Head of Indigenous Engagement and Strategy with the National Gallery of Australia, Cara has previously worked with the Department of Parliamentary Services, Creative Australia, AGSA's Tarnanthi Festival and Desart in Mparntwe (Alice Springs).

JAX BROWN (they/them) is an esteemed disability and LGBTIQA+ rights activist, writer, educator and consultant. Their tireless commitment to LGBTIQA+ disability human rights and advocacy has been recognised with a Medal of the Order of Australia (OAM). Jax utilises their experience as a queer, trans wheelchair user to explore intersectional identities.

The Relationship is the Project

A guide to working with communities

Edited by
Jade Lillie and Kate Larsen
with Cara Kirkwood and Jax Brown

NEWSOUTH

UNSW Press acknowledges the Bedegal people, the Traditional Owners of the unceded territory on which the Randwick and Kensington campuses of UNSW are situated, and recognises their continuing connection to Country and culture. We pay our respects to Bedegal Elders past and present.

A NewSouth book

Published by
NewSouth Publishing
University of New South Wales Press Ltd
University of New South Wales
Sydney NSW 2052
AUSTRALIA
https://unsw.press/

A catalogue record for this book is available from the National Library of Australia

ISBN   9781742238234 (paperback)
        9781742238982 (ebook)
        9781742239941 (ePDF)

Internal design Josephine Pajor-Markus
Cover design Regine Abos
Cover illustration Clive Watts/Stocksy
Printer Griffin Press

This book has been designed and typeset with the intention of being accessible to as many different users as possible.

This book is printed on paper using fibre supplied from plantation or sustainably managed forests.

Australian Government

Creative Australia

Contents

Acknowledgement

The Relationship is the Project was written and edited on unceded land.

We acknowledge First Peoples as the first artists, the first storytellers, the first communities and the first creators of culture, and the Traditional Owners and Elders whose stories and experiences are the heart of the lands on which our contributors live and work:

- Boorloo (Perth) and Walyalup (Fremantle) – Noongar
- Castlemaine and Hepburn Springs – Dja Dja Wurrung
- Darling Downs – Jarrowair
- Gimuy (Cairns) – Gimuy Walubarra Yidinji and Yirrganydji
- Darwin – Larrakia
- Lutruwita (Tasmania) – Palawa
- Meanjin (Brisbane) – Turrbul and Jagera
- Mount Gambier – Boandik
- Mulgoa (Western Sydney) – Dharug
- Naarm (Melbourne) – Boon Wurrung, Bunurong, Woi Wurrung and Wurundjeri
- Ngambri/Ngunnawal (Canberra) – Ngunnawal
- Oakland, California (USA) – Ohlone
- Riverland – Ngaiawang, Ngawait, Nganguruku, Erawirung, Ngintait, Ngaralte and Ngarkat
- Rubibi (Broome) – Yawuru
- Tarntanya (Adelaide) – Kaurna
- Warrane/Cadi (Sydney) – Gadigal

We are grateful for all the First Nations artists and communities that we work alongside in solidarity, including those who have contributed to this project.

Aboriginal and Torres Strait Islander people are advised that this document may contain images of people who are deceased.

Welcome

Welcome to *The Relationship is the Project*.

This is a book of provocations, tools and practical tips for those who are currently working or are interested in working with communities. It is intended to be a solid starting point for organisations, project managers, artists, cultural workers and other community-engaged practitioners who want to bring new perspectives and ideas to their work.

This project began as a response to growing interest in working better with communities, and in finding out how to develop relationships that foster creativity, cultural engagement and audiences. It aims to be an accessible text that is a place to start learning and return to when you want to know more. In it, you'll find wisdom from practitioners and thought leaders from across Australia, mostly working within the fields of arts, culture and community development (though their learnings can be applied across a range of sectors and contexts).

Community-engaged practice is not an art form. It's not an add-on. It's a way of working: a deep collaboration between practitioners and communities to develop outcomes specific to that relationship, time and place. It is social, cultural, environmental and political, and can be used as a framework to tell stories, explore issues, and deliver beautiful and powerful projects. It can be used to shape the narratives of our time – as communities, as artists and as citizens.

This second edition responds to the local and global crises and challenges we've all experienced since the book's initial release, and the ongoing impacts of social isolation, increasing online engagement and new opportunities for world building. It felt timely to invite contributors to update existing chapters and commission 12 new works that we hope will again shift the dial on how we understand working with communities.

Whether reading about climate adaptation, disaster recovery, digital engagement or class, we will always have more questions than answers. We hope this book provides an entry point and guide into community-engaged practice.

This book is for you: the readers, practitioners, the people doing this work. Stay curious, don't assume; learn and re-learn. Share knowledge, open doors and keep them open. Change happens because we make it so.

What is community-engaged practice?

Jade Lillie

A community can be any geographically connected group of people, cultural group, young people, or anyone with a shared language, interest, campaign or lived experience.

It's important to remember that most people belong to more than one (check out the chapter on intersectionality for more).

What do we mean by 'community-engaged practice'?

'Community-engaged practice' is, at its simplest, a way of talking about how we work with communities. It has also been known as:

- community arts
- community engagement
- community cultural development (CCD)
- community arts and cultural development (CACD)
- social practice
- participatory practice
- community-engaged, contemporary arts practice.

From 'CCD' to 'CACD' and old-fashioned 'community arts', not having a shared terminology means that the sector has not had a united message, voice or set of principles for this work.

Fellow editor of this book and Australian cultural consultant Kate Larsen notes:

> 'Community-engaged practice' has emerged as a contemporary alternative to 'community arts and cultural development'. The term helps encapsulate non-creative as well as creative outcomes (even if those outcomes are achieved using art as a tool), avoids the negative connotations of 'community arts', and provides a distinction from 'community-led practice' for organisations that are not majority-led or governed by the communities they represent.

The heart of community-engaged practice is collaboration. It's not something we do to communities, but something we do together. Ideally, this is self-determined and ensures leadership at a community level.

It's used in situations where people come together around an issue or an idea with the aim of realising an outcome. This could be a project, a campaign, a new idea or a set of relationships being built for future opportunities.

Importantly, we rarely enter these sorts of collaborations with the idea that it is short-term or a one-off. Community-engaged practice is about our relationships with communities.

Process makes perfect

Community-engaged practice is an incredibly effective way to create great creative and cultural outcomes with artists, practitioners and communities. Key to its success is a solid process for the ways we work, inviting and ensuring input from communities and other stakeholders.

Start by thinking about the design of your project or experience in the following ways:

- Invitation. You don't have to wait for an invitation to start discussing an idea for a project, but it is very important that you are invited to continue to develop it. Ask the questions: Is this idea something that you would like to explore? Is this something we could do together? Be prepared to let it go if the answer is 'No'.
- Research. What has come before this conversation? It's unlikely you will be the first person, project or idea. Who was involved? Which organisations (arts and non-arts) have a history of working in this place/ space? Talk to them. Understand the current context as best you can without having to ask all of the same questions of the community members you are working with.
- Design. Some practitioners will design the project in collaboration with artists, participants and project partners (sometimes described as 'co-design'), while others will design a project themselves and take it to communities for input. Both ways are appropriate at different times – it really depends on the context. Ask people how they'd like to be involved and go from there.

- Delivery. Best-laid plans can (and do) change. The delivery stage needs to be the most flexible part of the process. Be open to change and redirection at all points.
- Outcome. Some practitioners believe that the outcome will not be known until the process is finished. Others (like myself) think you can generally know where it is heading and retain a willingness to shift when needed. The most important thing is that the outcome is something that everyone can be proud of, and that it has been given the time and expertise to become the best it can be. If the relationship or trust is damaged in pursuit of the outcome, this is considered an #EpicFail.
- Reflection. This is something we rarely make time for but is very important. Celebrate successes, find out if something hasn't gone well, and learn how to adapt when you next do something similar. Reflection should happen with all project stakeholders – artists and participants, colleagues and partners. It can come in the form of surveys, focus groups, sharing a meal with a community group, leading a structured conversation, or informal conversations with stakeholders. Build capacity for reflection into the design of the project.

What community-engaged practice is not

We've seen an increase in funding bodies, organisations and institutions interested in 'doing community engagement'. This suggests that it is something outside of or to be inflicted on a largely amorphous community, a thing we develop and then invite people to come along to. Let's be clear about what community-engaged practice is not:

✗ a one-off workshop to build audiences
✗ unpaid labour where communities are asked to share skills, expertise, intellectual or creative or cultural property without any remuneration or reciprocity
✗ an online focus group or survey
✗ an expert/specialist-led experience such as a residency or class where community members might 'learn a new skill'
✗ an activity designed to build a database or contact list.

Call something what it is: if it is a one-off workshop delivered by artists who are in town for a performance, then it is simply a workshop with artists, not 'community engagement'.

....

Things to keep in mind

* Listen. Often, this includes listening to things that are not being said. Non-verbal cues are also important to observe. Be patient.

* Maintain an interest and commitment to people being the visible 'face' of the project (other than yourself). This means you need to be happy to take a back seat and make sure other people have the opportunity to speak first.

* Have a clear agenda. There are many reasons for using a community-engaged framework, but it is important that you are clear and upfront about your own agenda. Is it because it is simply your job? Or because you received investment for a 'community engagement' element in the project? Is it your organisation's mission and vision? Or are you trying to move into a more engaged practice framework for your next work? Whatever the reason, be clear and honest.

* Remember that you're being paid. This 'payment' could be through a grant or organisation or even through your choice to volunteer on a project. It doesn't matter what or how much you're getting paid. You are still receiving some kind of benefit to lead or work on an initiative. This will not be the case for the people you are working with (unless they are being paid to participate). This can create a power imbalance, so it is important to be clear about what this means for all of the stakeholders involved.

* Hone your facilitation and communication skills. These develop over time, but you'll need to be a great communicator to be a great facilitator.

* Be flexible. Things will change and shift throughout the project. Whether you're dealing with a change in direction, location, timeline or creative team, flexibility is key.

* Allow enough time. Collaboration always takes more time than you anticipate. This is particularly important when engaging with a new community. Take the time; meet the right people; make the connections that will develop the idea. This means it can be difficult to be part of multiple community-engaged projects at the same time (unless you are part of an organisation or team).

* Develop excellent organisational skills. If you're not organised, your project is unlikely to be a good experience for you or the communities you are working with. It is very important to respect the time of the people participating in the project. By being organised, you are being respectful. Work with other people who can provide the skills you lack.

* Know yourself. What are you good at? What are your flaws? What are your biases and how do they impact the way you work? Are you racially literate and culturally competent? What don't you know? What are the skills and capabilities you bring to this project and what are your gaps?

* Ask, don't assume. Making assumptions is one of the ways we cut corners in community-engaged contexts. Even if you have been working with a group of artists or communities for a long time, it's important that you continue to ask questions and clarify that you are on the right track.

* Reflect. Make sure you take the time to evaluate throughout, to reflect and assess. What would you do differently? What worked well? Celebrate the successes and leave the door open for the next conversation.

First Peoples first

Genevieve Grieves

There is a movement in the arts and cultural sectors to place First Peoples first. This call for action is in response to nearly 250 years of inaction – an ongoing inability to right the wrongs of the past – to create a just and equal society that gives all its citizens an opportunity to survive and flourish. People in our sector recognise the need to create positive social change and do the work of anti-racism and decolonisation through cultural safety and meaningful collaboration.

Colonisation: a moving frontier

It is important to recognise that there are a range of First Peoples communities across urban, regional and remote Australia. This continent is a rich tapestry of over 250 different nations that have their own law, arts, culture and language, and their own experiences of colonisation.

I use the term 'First Peoples' rather than 'Aboriginal' or 'Indigenous' as it is the preferred term in the community (Narrm/Melbourne) where I have lived for the past 20 years. 'Aboriginal' is a generic term that does not reflect our sovereignty or diversity; 'Indigenous' is equally generic but does connect the mainland to the Torres Strait Islands and our struggles and experience with groups in other countries who also consider themselves 'Indigenous'.

The colonisation of this country, now known as Australia, was not an event that happened in 1770 and ended there. The English laid claim to the continent in 1770, but invasion occurred as a 'moving frontier', with some First Peoples in the centre of the continent not meeting settlers until the 1980s.

However, colonisation also needs to be understood as a structure, and not an event that occurred at a certain time. Colonisation began here more than 200 years ago, but Australia continues to be both a colonised and actively colonising country. This reality has severe and ongoing impacts for the First Peoples of Australia. As diverse as we may be, all communities across the nation of Australia share experiences of colonisation: loss of land, massacre, removal of children, servitude, stolen wages, segregation and racism. These experiences have created deep trauma in communities that is rarely adequately addressed – leading to family violence, suicide, alcohol and substance abuse, homelessness and ill health.

It is difficult for communities to deal with the complex legacies and continuing realities of colonisation, particularly when they are reliant on external funding and policymaking support to do so. We are all under the whim and power of local, state and federal authorities whose political agendas and short-term vision do not coincide with the needs of our communities to heal and determine our own futures. Despite these challenges, there are many community success stories of resilience, adaptation and innovation across the country.

The role of arts and culture

Arts and culture play an integral role in the survival and future of our people.

As our cultures and communities are diverse, so is our art practice. Art has always connected us to the Ancestral world and shared our stories and culture. In more recent times, it has recorded and shared our experiences of colonisation and been used as a political tool to demand justice and change. Art is also a lifeline for many communities, providing opportunities for economic survival.

Our arts and cultural practice is embedded in an 'arts industry' and is a valuable commodity supporting a large sector. Within this sector are many allies who work with communities to create opportunity and social change, but there are also people and practices that have had and continue to have negative impacts. This includes 'fake art' (non-Indigenous people creating Indigenous art) and paternalistic practices.

The role of allies

When working in First Peoples contexts, the most important relationship for an interested worker-for-change is relationship to self. There are many non-Indigenous people working in this space. Their relationships with communities can range from paternalistic and colonising to allies who are supportive of community aspirations. Many come with a range of their own issues that can make it difficult for them to be effective allies.

Understand your own position

As a member of Australian society, you need to understand who you are in relation to this land and its people. Many Australians do not know their nation's origin story and their relationship to a sovereign country that was never ceded. Ask yourself where you have come from, where your country is, when your Ancestors came to this place and what their interactions were with the First Peoples of this land.

This positioning is part of moving beyond the denial many Australians experience in their understanding of Indigenous people and shared history. Denial is a very strong part of Australian culture. It is a resistance to embracing the difficult truths of invasion and genocide because of feelings of guilt and shame.

Recognise and understand your own culture

If you are not white, culture will probably be an easy concept for you to understand. But for white Australians, this can be more elusive. As whiteness is normalised and made neutral, white people do not often understand that they have a culture. When working in a different cultural space – that of First Peoples communities, for example – they recognise the difference of the culture they see before them, but not the culture they bring with them. This can make it difficult for them to operate effectively in First Peoples' cultural spaces, as they are unaware of the way their culture influences their own actions.

Recognise your privilege

Privilege can be afforded in many different forms. Fair skin, level of education, language proficiency, or access to resources can create privilege for an individual in this society. Having privilege can make you an effective ally and tool for social change, in that you can use your privilege to support community aspirations. However, it can also mean that you are not used to putting others' needs before your own. It can lead to a belief that you know better than others because of your experience as a privileged person.

Decolonise your practice

Colonisation is evident at every level of our society: within our legal, education and political systems; our institutions; the food we eat; how we interact with one another; and in the ways that we act and think. It is not just the First Peoples of this land who are colonised. Some argue that all members of a colonised society need to decolonise themselves and the spaces they intersect with.

Yet, decolonising a society really means to return land to First Peoples, to right the wrong of invasion and dispossession. This is unlikely to occur in contexts such as Australia. Instead, decolonisation can be viewed as a tool to make visible the impacts and reach of colonisation and to work out ways to dismantle it.

Very few spaces are decolonised, so there is much work to be done to consciously and actively create these. This can include centring First Peoples culture in a project so that it isn't built on or in support of Western frameworks, but strengthens First Peoples' knowledge and ways of doing. Or ensuring that First Peoples are strongly represented within the power structures and decision-making process, whether this includes a board or steering committee or (ideally) a cultural governance structure.

However, the first step towards decolonisation is being able to recognise and identify how colonialism works. Read texts, connect with others in the space, and critically engage with the world around you. These are some useful resources to start your decolonising journey:

- *Decolonizing Methodologies* by New Zealand professor of education and Māori development Linda Tuhuwai Smith
- *Another Day in the Colony* by Mununjali Yugambeh and South Sea Islander woman and professor of Indigenous health Chelsea Watego
- *Decolonizing Solidarity* by academic and researcher Clare Land
- *Reports from a Wild Country: Ethics for Decolonisation* by ethnographer Deborah Bird Rose.

There are so many incredible First Nations content creators you can connect with on social media, including Common Ground, who have an online archive that you can use to educate yourself about history and contemporary issues.

Working in First Peoples contexts

As an interested worker-for-change, you can make a huge difference by committing yourself to working with First Peoples communities. There are many success stories of non-Indigenous allies and advocates who have made ongoing positive impacts in their work.

There are also people who engage with communities in a problematic way. The great interest in and appetite for First Peoples arts and culture means there are people looking for an experience or career development rather than wanting to support social justice and change. Others can be driven by a desire to reduce feelings of guilt and bring their emotional issues into spaces where there is already a range of issues to deal with.

This not only further complicates matters for communities but also means that important support roles are filled with people who are ineffective, or even damaging. Some are paternalistic and, while they may do good work in developing community opportunities and projects, are not willing to let go of their power and hand the reins over to the community.

Understanding your own relationship to this country and our shared history is key to being effective in these spaces, as is developing meaningful and equal relationships with First Peoples communities. Ideally, this should be a long-term commitment. Allow time to understand the unique and complex experience of each community and its continuing work to decolonise, survive and thrive.

....

Things to keep in mind

* Know yourself and your culture. What beliefs/
  practices are you bringing into this work?
  Understand your own culture and cultural practice.
  If applicable, recognise your white privilege and how
  your whiteness operates internally and externally.
* Understand the unique history and culture of a place.
  Each First Peoples community is different. Spend
  time learning and understanding the local context.
* Work yourself out of a job. Create opportunities to
  strengthen and support local mob to take over your
  position.
* Don't think you know best. Communities have the
  answers to their own problems.
* Learn from the past. Listen and learn about what
  has gone before. Support community aspirations and
  existing projects rather than reinventing the wheel.
* Do not speak for First Peoples. Always know your
  place as a supporter and an ally, not as a leader.
* Make a long-term commitment. The longer you work
  with a community, the greater your understanding
  and the more effective you will be.
* Take time to build trust. Communities have
  experienced many workers come and go, with a range
  of positive and negative experiences. There have also
  been many disappointments due to broken promises
  and policy failures. Take the time you need to prove
  your worth.

....

Cultural safety: Beyond inclusion

Ruth De Souza

In the wake of Black Lives Matter, deaths in custody and calls to decolonise or indigenise, individuals, groups and organisations are under increasing pressure to demonstrate their accountability for responding to racism. However, well-intentioned diversity, equity and inclusion (DEI) initiatives often (re)produce the same exclusion and inequity they are trying to undo because they assume the presence of 'others' means that they have power, and they neglect race, social justice and safety.

Why diversity, equity and inclusion aren't enough

The concept of 'diversity' was originally introduced as a social justice mechanism to broaden participation and access for groups who had been marginalised. It is based on the idea that diversity is intrinsically valuable. Unfortunately, diversity, equity and inclusion approaches centre white-settler norms. In focusing on 'others' as a problem or deficit, they promote inclusion into a (typically) white norm as a remedy, without any structural changes.

DEI approaches rest on the assumption that the long shadows of colonialism have been resolved and settler–Indigenous relationships are equal. Thus, the presence of 'diverse' people in organisations is seen as evidence of the organisation's inclusiveness.

Critics of DEI initiatives note that because they rarely include language like 'racism', 'white supremacy' or 'anti-Blackness', they can be apolitical and do not get to the heart of the actual problem of injustice.

What is cultural safety?

In contrast, the concept of 'cultural safety' demands intentional self and organisational critique to look at how our behaviours, opinions and actions as people who work within institutions can negatively affect the cultural identity and wellbeing of the people we work with. Cultural safety offers arts, cultural and community workers the opportunity to examine how unquestioned ways of doing things can be barriers for groups to engage with us. Individuals and organisations can also use the idea to reflect on their work and address imbalances of power through building equal partnerships.

How is cultural safety relevant to the cultural and community sectors?

Cultural safety not only recognises the validity of beliefs and practices of people and communities that may differ from our own, but also challenges us to act to make spaces safer. As arts and cultural workers, we can use this approach to ensure that we do not impose our own values and beliefs in ways that result in a loss of power for others.

Where does 'cultural safety' come from?

The term was originally taken up by the Nursing Council of New Zealand (NCNZ) in 1992 in response to advocacy from Māori nurses, in particular Irihapeti Ramsden. The nurses wanted to make sure the cultural identities of Māori people were respected by health professionals and organisations that were knowingly and/or unknowingly biased towards non-Māori people and practices.

According to NCNZ, cultural safety now refers to both an ethical framework and its intended outcome, in which the person delivering a service 'will have undertaken a process of reflection on their own cultural identity and will recognise the impact that their personal culture has on their professional practice'.

This is based on a definition of culture that goes beyond race. 'Culture includes, but is not restricted to age or generation, gender, sexual orientation, occupation and socioeconomic status, ethnic origin or migrant experience, religious or spiritual belief, and disability … Unsafe cultural practice comprises any action which diminishes, demeans or disempowers the cultural identity and wellbeing of an individual.'

When we build upon this idea in non-health contexts, it is important to be respectful and recognise cultural safety's history and original intent. Cultural safety is an Indigenous peoples' approach strengthened by over 25 years of development.

Cultural safety helps us develop different ways of thinking and talking about discrimination, and then act to effect change. It helps us draw attention to and combat the effects of dominant culture bias in our institutions and identify how this impacts the diversity of the arts and cultural sector.

A cultural safety approach also provides a consistent language that can be used across our sector at any level (not just in community-engaged practice).

Why do we need cultural safety?

Australia is a white settler colony, in which British invasion and colonisation have institutionalised whiteness. Like other sectors, this history is strongly reflected in the arts, including the ways our practitioners, organisations and institutions develop and deliver projects in collaboration with artists and communities. Arts organisations often unconsciously prioritise and centre whiteness. For people and communities who are not white, these organisations may not be seen as appropriate, accessible or acceptable, which can prevent participation and engagement.

A 2020 report from Australia Council for the Arts (now known as Creative Australia) shows that the arts and cultural sector does not currently reflect the socially, culturally and politically diverse contemporary society within which we all live.

- First Nations people are under-represented in the cultural and creative workforce and 56 per cent of multi-year investment organisations have no First Nations people in leadership roles.

- There is low representation of culturally and linguistically diverse (CALD) Australians in cultural leadership roles and among grant recipients, and Australians from non-English-speaking backgrounds are under-represented among artists.
- Disabled artists earn 42 per cent less and are more likely to be unemployed than their non-disabled peers. Disabled people make up just 3 per cent of cultural leaders within multi-year investment organisations.
- There are just as many women artists in Australia as men, but women earn 30 per cent less for creative work and 25 per cent less overall. There are additional inequalities for women artists whose identities intersect with other areas of diversity.
- Regionally based artists are paid a third less for creative work and are under-represented in the cultural and creative workforce.
- Younger Australians make up just 5 per cent of artists in Australia, 3 per cent of successful grant applicants, and are under-represented in the cultural and creative workforce. People under 35 years have low representation in almost all cultural leadership roles, except creative leadership roles.
- The artist population is older than the Australian workforce: almost one in five artists is aged 65 years or over (18 per cent). However, few people aged over 65 apply for grants or hold cultural leadership positions.

The arts sector can be as racist, ableist, transphobic, homophobic, classist, ageist and sexist as our broader society. Cultural safety requires us to be conscious of the whole context within which we operate, and to work across historically isolated categories of difference.

As Melbourne writer and arts worker Andy Butler observes:

> Staying sane as a person of colour in the arts in Australia means being able to hold two oppositional ideas as simultaneously true. One is that there is a community of Black, Indigenous and People of Colour in the arts who are doing important and incredible work. The other is that the sector is aggressively and institutionally White.

In this context, cultural safety has the potential to address the ongoing harm caused by colonisation in order to address racism and improve outcomes for Aboriginal and Torres Strait Islander people (and beyond). Cultural safety also has the potential to transform institutional responses to these statistics. It is a stakeholder-centred approach that emphasises sharing decision-making, information, power and responsibility.

Cultural safety opportunities

Cultural safety offers a well-developed language and layered approach for practitioners to critically reflect, discuss and act on issues of privilege, power and difference. In doing so, it connects individual actions to broad-based approaches to systemic change. It supports reflection between cultures and experiences, but also within cultural groups. And it is broad enough to recognise issues and concerns across a range of individual and collective experiences and creative practices, enabling an intersectional approach to the challenges we face as a sector.

Cultural safety can be put into action by applying its principles to our work. Health educators Kerry Taylor and Pauline Thompson Guerin adapted the work of Māori nurse educator Irihapeti Ramsden to identify four core principles of cultural safety:

1   Practise critical self-reflection: as part of an ongoing process of developing our understanding of ourselves. In particular, we need to commit to increasing our awareness of the way we see the world and how our identity and the groups we belong to are formed and influenced by history, society and the context in which we live.

2   Use engaged communication: with the commitment to accepting another person's point of view, not making assumptions, and approaching difference with equity rather than judgment. It is particularly important in culturally safe communication not to speak or act on behalf of anyone else.

3   Minimise power imbalances: by developing an awareness of power, how power can be different in each new context, and how we can take appropriate action to share power with those we are working with. Employment can give us different types of power such as access to funds and equipment but it can also give us status and authority.

4   Decolonise practice: by identifying and changing parts of our work such as language, processes and structures that reinforce colonising processes. 'Decolonising' does not only refer to the historical events of colonisation but to the processes of domination or control of one group over another.

Things to keep in mind

We cannot declare ourselves to be culturally safe. Instead, our work is identified as culturally safe or unsafe by the people we work with. Don't wait for someone to lead you towards cultural safety. Take responsibility, do the work yourself, and then go beyond individual attitudes to collective practices:

*   Understand and get to know your own biases through reflection. Consider how your own cultural background structures your thinking and behaviour.
*   Be curious about your reactions. Explore the fragility, discomfort, guilt, defensiveness or resistance that may arise and be willing to learn from it.
*   Read and research. There are plenty of books, blogs, articles and websites on cultural safety and related areas that invite us to reflect on our biases and worldviews as well as the ways power and control operate. These include critical whiteness, racial literacy, queer theory, ableism, intersectionality, decolonisation and feminism.
*   Attend workshops, talks, events and conferences. Expand your appreciation and respect for people whose experience and knowledge differ from your own.
*   Self-evaluate and invite peer evaluation of your arts activities, projects and practice. Ask yourself how you have applied cultural safety principles to your work and what actions you have taken to address culturally unsafe spaces within your sphere of influence.

* Find or develop a community of practice. This may be a network, a small group, or even a few friends you can meet in a safe space to discuss the ideas and principles behind cultural safety. This is a group where you can collectively draw on each other's skills and knowledge, brainstorm, challenge and support each other's ongoing development.
* Commit to communicating about cultural safety and the lack of it with those you work with.
* Use your privilege and access to resources to examine and challenge organisations, institutions and structures. Think about the values and ways of working that are evident in the arts and cultural organisations you engage with. Amplify the values that reflect cultural safety, and challenge and disrupt those that do not.
* Lead, steward and/or support your organisation towards a commitment (and actions) to being a culturally safe place.
* Above all, persist. Working towards cultural safety in your creative practice is a lifelong commitment. Acknowledge and celebrate the effort and the learnings along the way.

••

The original version of this chapter was co-written with Robyn Higgins and published in the first edition of *The Relationship is the Project* (Brow Books, 2020).

Creatively and culturally safe spaces

Lia Pa'apa'a

Community-engaged practice is as much about the process as it is about the outcome. Ensuring culturally and creatively safe spaces means people are able to get the most out of what that process has to offer.

Creatively and culturally safe spaces are situations and places where a person can feel welcome, and that their cultural experiences and knowledge are respected and valued. They are spaces where people don't have to leave their cultures, kinships, family and ancestors at the door. They are spaces where the creative and cultural are intertwined as a way of being in the world.

Community-engaged projects often have cultural and community layers that arts organisations or institutions have to manage. These layers are often the essence and strength of a project, but can also present new complexities. Creating culturally and creative safe spaces requires strong, trusting working relationships.

Know yourself

To be a successful community-engaged practitioner, it is important to recognise your own story first. Your relationship with yourself and your story is fundamental to your practice and, therefore, your projects. Each of us comes with our own learnt presumptions. It's important to ensure that we are aware of these and how, as practitioners, they will impact our work to build creative and culturally safe spaces.

What is your role within a project? What are the different experiences and understandings that you bring to that role? Knowing your lenses, strengths and weaknesses as a practitioner will help you build a space that puts the needs of the participants at the forefront of any project. If you don't feel that you have the skills to deliver a project, then seek help or step back (so you don't do more damage than good).

Creating safe spaces

Creating culturally and creatively safe spaces isn't easy. Complexities often emerge as a project develops. As the facilitator of that project, you need to be across all of the following areas of development and delivery.

Planning

Community-engaged projects must be built through a strength-based approach. Using the existing strengths of the people and places you're working with will allow you to create projects that are unique, engaged and valued by participants in their own community context. To identify some of the existing strengths of a place or community, consider the following questions:

- Who lives in the community? What are the skills/ expertise that can be accessed from within it?

- What cultural protocols or frameworks can be built into a project that support what you are trying to achieve?
- What are the local organisations in the area?
  Is there any overlap with the work you are doing?
  Can partnerships be forged?

Self-care

Being a community-engaged practitioner can often be all encompassing. There are many ups and downs. Energy is required on physical, emotional, cultural and, sometimes, spiritual levels.

It's important to look after yourself throughout the life of any project. This should be built into each project from its inception. Make self-care a priority at the development stage by asking the following kinds of questions:

- Are you dealing with complex and challenging content in the project? Does there need to be additional emotional and cultural support for yourself and/or the participants?
- How long will you be away from home? Do you need more travel budget to get home to loved ones periodically?
- What does the schedule look like? Can healthy meals, exercise and movement be built in?

Producing

Producing or managing a project is a large part of a facilitator's role. Often, a key reason why we are engaged is because the community does not have the skills to make sure the administration, resourcing and logistics of a project are secure.

Our role is to be the bridge between the creative and cultural content and the management of the project. This can include a lot of paperwork, systems, grant writing and data entry. It's rarely fun, but without it a great creative and cultural project can fall down.

Money story

It is essential to communicate clearly and openly about wages, fees and transactions to make sure everyone is happy to participate. Clear understanding of the money story allows people to understand the scope of the project and what is expected of them.

Being clear about fees and payment timelines can make people feel valued for their contributions. When this isn't done well, it can lead to a culture of suspicion and distrust, which undo all your hard work.

Succession planning

Many projects come and go from communities. But community-engaged practitioners have the chance to develop something that has a lasting impact. In order to do this, we have to recognise that projects are bigger than the individuals involved. This means that we must think about succession planning from the beginning of a project.

Unless you're working with your own community, the reality is that you will probably leave at some point. This literally means that from the day you start the project, you should be working yourself out of a job. At the very least, you should include training and capacity building within the project so that you're able to hand over elements to local participants. This makes room for locals to lead different elements of the project for themselves. This is important for making culturally and creatively safe spaces as it allows for learnt cultural knowledges and relationships to stay intact after any one individual leaves. As practitioners, it also means we can have diverse and fulfilling careers across projects and communities while knowing that the work we've done is being continued by people who value it.

Communication

When the core of your practice is about people and their stories, you get to work across art forms. Community-engaged practice takes place in film, music, traditional and contemporary dance, theatre, weaving, craft, gaming and more.

It's important to be able to communicate clearly what the project is about, and how it is going to be achieved, to a variety of stakeholders. This means that you need to be able to communicate to elders, children and community members as well as funders, organisations and other stakeholders.

Food

The social and cultural sharing of food is an important part of any community-engaged project. The layers of giving, nurturing, nourishing and storytelling that food provides can communicate the essence of a project without the need for words. A home-cooked meal can bring people together quickly and make participants feel supported and nourished.

- Consider the needs of the participants – are they new mothers or parents, elders or people with underlying health issues? Is there something that they would enjoy or that would nourish them in particular.
- Provide a dish from your own cultural heritage as a way of sharing a part of yourself and where you come from.
- Slow-cooker meals can be an easy, cheap and effective way to cater a warm meal.
- Keep it healthy – let your menu reflect the values of the project. Nourishing, nutritious and delicious meals show the level of care you are setting out to provide.

Creating culturally and creative safe spaces online

Since the pandemic, there has been a rise in online engagement and activity. For people living in regional or remote settings, parents of small children and people with access needs (to name a few), this has increased access to arts and culture in exciting new ways.

We can now work with hybrid models of engagement, which is an exciting opportunity to create more regular engagement while reducing travel costs and climate impacts, and which can lead to increasing direct support for artists and communities.

These are some ways to create meaningful engagement for your online groups:

- Set boundaries and protocols to keep the space safe.
- Provide a creative practice for people to do while online – this could be paying an artist to deliver a workshop or providing activities for people to do while listening to presentations. Post materials prior to online sessions so everyone has what they need.
- Cater online sessions by either sending out premade snacks, vouchers to local stores or ingredients to cook together.
- Build self-care into online sessions such as breath work, movement or guided meditations.
- Create a community outside of the online session. this could be an online group chat to allow people to connect in their own way, share resources and continue conversations after the session is finished.

Small gestures can show a level of care and set the tone for the online sessions that allow shared moments to happen in real time and create an embodied connection of food, movement and play (rather than just a screen of talking heads).

Legacy

One way of measuring the impact of your work is to think about the legacy you are leaving behind – for the project, communities and individuals involved.

Creating culturally and creatively safe spaces is multi-faceted and complex, often achieved by working across a broad range of stakeholders and areas. This means the legacy of a project can be far reaching. By developing a positive legacy, you leave behind foundations and frameworks for future projects that the community can work from.

Legacies can exist in three ways:

- Creative. Do your collaborators have a better understanding of how they can create and deliver their work to the wider sector? This could include developing pathways to other organisations or opportunities, taking people to shows to be inspired, mentorships or networking.
- Logistical. What physical resources has the project left behind? This could include things such as structures, power sources, staging or equipment that could be used for other events in the future.
- Human. Has the project given people in the community the skills to deliver their own projects? Have you created practical and simple systems and templates for the community to use?

Reciprocity

Community-engaged practice is embedded in reciprocity. As practitioners, we are often given the honour and privilege to learn, see, hear and feel people's experiences and stories. We are trusted with practices, processes and stories that can sometimes be literally on the brink of extinction.

It is important that we have the capacity and skill set to deliver what is best for the project, and that we do our best to ensure our participants' cultural and creative needs are at the forefront. This is what we give back to them. We give the best practice framework for them to work within. We ensure that they are safe to explore, grow and create.

Things to keep in mind

* Learning about your participants and their community allows you to build the project from a strength-based approach, acknowledging and respecting all the knowledge systems and hard work that has come before you, while also allowing you to capitalise on resources.
* Think about the layers of advisory and community engagement you need to have to make a project work (such as input from Elders, youth, or local organisations).
* Think about what outcomes are achievable and who has the capacity to deliver them.

Racial literacy: What is 'race' and why is it so important to understand?

Dianne Jones, Odette Kelada and Lilly Brown

Race is an idea invented to divide and oppress. Understanding that is the start of racial literacy.

Racial literacy is not a checklist to tick off, a unit of study to complete or a goal to achieve. There is no end to learning to be racially literate. It is the continuous process of getting educated about all of the ways race has shaped and is shaped by ongoing colonisation and power relations.

People have a lot of opinions about race, but often don't know how or when the current idea of race came about, its connection to power relations or its impact. Conversations about race that happen without this sort of informed context often rehash racist stereotypes heard around the home, in school or through mainstream news sources.

Learning racial literacy is about getting educated on the history, meanings and lived experiences connected with the word 'race' and other critical terms that flow from it – racism, whiteness, supremacy, privilege.

This learning requires reflexive practices – asking yourself about your ways of thinking, seeing, believing, behaving and feeling about race. This learning is about acquiring tools to understand why race representation matters.

In our experience teaching about race, we have witnessed people feel empowered after actively beginning to develop their racial literacy practice (Brown, Kelada & Jones, 2021). Racial literacy enables people to move beyond a moral stand against racism to an informed one.

This empowerment is a vital first step to decoding the legacies of ideas about race that are used to justify exploitation, punitive treatment and neglect of human rights.

How much does race affect your life?

How racially literate you are will affect your answer to this question and your understanding of race and racial literacy. As one white student said to us in the context of their experience undertaking a subject underpinned by a racial literacy framework: 'While I knew I was raced, I didn't think as much of it, and I didn't notice it as much.' (Brown et al., 2021). If you think 'race' has little to do with you or is not your 'problem', then it's most likely that you were brought up white.

Race theorist Richard Dyer notes that 'as long as race is something only applied to non-white people ... they/we function as a human norm. Other people are raced, we are just white'.

Race has been created as a category for the 'other' – the problem of the 'other' and the 'other' as the problem. Whiteness is assumed as the 'norm'. As a result, many white people may think that getting educated about race is about studying the 'other'. But everyone in any room is 'raced'. Often when white people first learn about race, and whiteness as a racialised concept and experience, it is a light bulb moment.

Race and privilege

Ideals of everyone having a 'fair go' and being able to 'succeed' on individual merit is known as the myth of meritocracy. This myth can be dangerous without an understanding of the histories of racial oppression and injustices that embed racial inequality into systems and institutions.

The idea of 'privilege' is not a vague term or indication of something inherently positive. It is a way of talking about whiteness as a historic, legal racial category linked to laws that gave privileges – rights, power and wealth – to people identified as 'white' at the expense of others. A racial literacy approach builds a toolkit for understanding and explaining the language and history of this privilege, and the lived experience of race and racism today.

'Race' categories

Racial literacy requires education on when and how categories of race were invented as a classification system for humans.

The power of race is that categories of humans were invented but made to appear as though they were biologically 'real' (through scientific racism), and placed in a hierarchy from superior to inferior. But there is no 'race' gene that is the same in all members of a 'race'. This myth conceals the fact that race categories justified the labelling of non-white people as inherently

less intelligent, lazy, criminal, deviant and able to be
exploited.

Racial literacy through the arts

Drawing on creative arts through visual images
and popular culture can be a powerful way to get
conversations on racial literacy started. In her 2000
artwork *Shearing the Rams*, Dianne Jones removes
the white shearers who are centred in the famous
Australian painting of the same name and replaces
them with images of her own father and brother
who also worked in shearing sheds. In doing so, she
brings attention through art to colonial histories and
how Aboriginal labour and exploitation have been
erased from stories of Australian nation building.

Shearing the Rams by Dianne Jones

Racial literacy approaches:
What good practice looks like

Writing on racial literacy emerged in America in 2004 through the work of Lani Guinier and France Winddance Twine.

Guinier, a legal scholar, civil rights lawyer, author, and the first woman of colour to obtain a position as a tenure-track professor at Harvard University, defines her approach in her examination of why there is still a gap between black and white students' education in America, despite the racial desegregation laws of 1954.

Professor of sociology, ethnographer, documentary filmmaker and feminist race theorist Twine defines racial literacy through exploring racial dynamics and education in inter-racial families and relationships. Twine's criteria for racial literacy provides some key elements for good practice:

- a recognition of whiteness, so it is no longer invisible or the 'norm'
- the definition of racism as a current social problem rather than just a historic legacy
- an understanding that racial identities are learnt and are an outcome of social processes – this means they can be 'unlearned'
- a vocabulary and language that facilitates a discussion of race and racism
- the ability to see and translate racial codes and practices
- an analysis of the ways racism intersects with class inequalities, gender hierarchies and heteronormativity.

....

Things to keep in mind

✳   First Nations histories and voices are core to
    racial literacy practices. Understanding impacts of
    Indigenous dispossession and ongoing colonisation
    is foundational.

✳   Positionality is critical. Often the only ones who
    talk about their racial position are People of Colour
    and Indigenous peoples. This keeps whiteness as
    'invisible' and appearing as though somehow outside
    'race' rather than the invented apex of the racial
    hierarchy.

✳   Think about who the 'I' is in your 'we'. Using 'we' in
    a way that assumes those who are listening are white
    can keep ideas of whiteness as the 'norm' in place.

✳   Ask yourself: Who is at the centre of the
    conversation? Who is taking up or giving up space
    in the conversation? Who is silent? What does
    silence do?

✳   Explore how everyone's personal story is shaped
    by the story of race. Connect the past with this
    moment and trace the connections. How have laws
    and policies on citizenship, immigration, housing,
    education, health and inheritance impacted
    generations?

✳   Build and disseminate your own resources on
    race education. For those who identify as white,
    do not expect education from People of Colour or
    Indigenous people.

✳   Systems in place over many years can appear neutral,
    but they're often not. What changes would have an
    impact on systems, habits and practices (such as

changing your employment policy and ideas of 'merit' versus equal representation)?

* Yes, race is a construct, but also real, lived experiences. This knowledge of race as 'invented' is not a reason to dismiss the need for racial literacy and education.

* Keep race on the table. Avoid the tendency to divert to another topic or re-centre whiteness. Bringing race and whiteness into the room makes for uncomfortable conversations. Practise the ability to stay 'uncomfortable' if this is new to you.

* Check in with emotions continually. The stories of race are not abstract, as they are also your story. Breathe and feel. Notice ego. Notice when you need a break and proper care. Notice if that break becomes an absence. Avoidance can also be an exercise of privilege for those who can leave and return to seeing race as a problem about/for the 'other'.

Intersectionality in community

Alia Gabres

The term 'intersectionality' was first used in a Black feminist context in 1989 by American academic and activist Kimberlé Williams Crenshaw. It was originally used as a way to understand how racial oppression had affected the Black community – most specifically the experience of Black women. More broadly, intersectionality is now used to show how some identities are marginalised, erased and discriminated against by systems and institutions. This includes anyone who is not considered 'mythically normal' (as per American writer and feminist Audre Lorde's definition), which means anyone who is not 'white, thin, male, young, heterosexual, Christian, and financially secure'.

It's also used to highlight the points where the politics of those identities overlap to multiply institutional discrimination, erasure or marginalisation (such as the effects of being both black and female, two distinct experiences that have historically led to compounded, institutionalised oppression)

Applying an intersectional lens

How can Black feminist theory be of use to us in the work of community, culture and creativity?

The arts are where we can collectively reimagine who we want to be. But in order to get to that future, we have to first deal with the realities of who we are. As artists, producers or cultural workers, it is our job to understand identity in the way Crenshaw describes it: 'not just a self-contained unit but a relationship between people and history, people and community, people and institutions'.

This is the basis of creating a whole-person framework for creative engagement. Working within an intersectional framework requires us to be open to the many parts of people's experiences, histories, identities and how they intersect. We are then called upon to develop programming that embodies those experiences.

The ability to identify and address inequities within a whole-person framework is what defines intersectional, community-engaged practice. In Melbourne, examples of whole-person frameworks can be seen in innovative programming such as:

- Community Reading Room's pop-up destination for research, community, discussion and engagement around art, culture and identity, which creates a space where the knowledge and research of Black and Indigenous People of Colour (BIPOC) can be centred and not relegated to the status of 'other' or 'diverse'
- the Moroccan Soup Bar's 'Speed date a Muslim' initiative, where nothing is off the table and Muslim women control the political narrative.

Practitioners like these use an intersectional lens to understand the structural impacts of issues affecting the communities they work with (such as racism, sexism or Islamophobia). Through this understanding, they have been able to create a way that addresses the harms caused by these outdated systems (such as marginalisation, discrimination and erasure).

When we work in a community-engaged context, our fundamental business is human interaction. If you're not interested in people, this work may not be for you. But if you're curious about how creativity can be the bridge to a place of human knowing and connection, then it may.

At times, your main responsibility will be to listen. At other times, you will be called on to use your expertise in service of the process. The key is to maintain an open and generous approach that is reflexive and accountable.

Black History Month: A case study in intersectionality

I now live in the United States, where February is Black History Month. It was created by Dr Carter G Woodson to highlight the histories and experiences of Black Americans. As part of my work, I was recently asked to join a group of literacy workers for a primary school 'read in' event organised by the school district and hosted by a number of local schools.

The picture book I selected was a favourite of mine, based on an Afro-Latina child's experience of belonging and migration. But as I waited with the other readers, I had the daunting feeling that it wasn't the right fit for a Black History Month event – it did not highlight the historical or lived experiences of Black Americans with an ancestral

---

connection to forcibly enslaved peoples. The reader sitting beside me attempted to give me some comfort about my choice. 'I wouldn't worry about it because the book you chose is about an Afro-Latina character so really it is intersectional', she said. 'She is black. It still counts.'

However, without a historical understanding of the nuances and intersections between the Afro-Latino and Black American experiences, what we risked doing was playing at being intersectional. By not presenting the story with the appropriate context, the intersections between both cultures were erased and the power that could have been built on the collectiveness of those experiences was diluted. Context matters.

Everyday intersections

Though we may come across diversity at the supermarket, gym, staff tearoom, or on the train, we don't often stop to think about how race, gender, sexuality, disability or class may show up in our daily interactions – especially in our work as cultural practitioners.

The following questions highlight how everyday experiences may be better understood through an intersectional lens:

- How does class and socio-economic status affect the quality of fresh produce available in your neighbourhood?

- How does race or gender affect the pay gap between you and your colleague in the staff tearoom?
- How do disability and binary gender 'norms' make access to basic facilities at your local gym difficult?
- How does race, socio-economic status or disability make access to some of our cultural institutions difficult or impossible?

Intersectionality and the institution

Can we apply an intersectional lens to arts and cultural institutions? The short answer is that we must.

Some of the most important work of intersectionality requires us to identify where longstanding institutional power lies. To see how that relates to the arts and cultural sectors, let's apply the 'mythically normal' test: are our arts and cultural institutions primarily made up of, and/or are they catering to, those who are 'white, thin, male, young, heterosexual, Christian, and financially secure'? If five of these seven descriptions apply, then we must concede that our institutions are in urgent need of repair.

The consequences of such structural problems within our institutions can be seen in communities that are disengaged or mistrustful of the institutions at best, or that experience marginalisation, discrimination or erasure at worst. In applying an intersectional lens to the problem, one may be tempted to use diversity as an answer, whether in increasing diverse programming, increasing diversity hire quotas, or adopting a diverse audience development strategy. However, these solutions often become temporary bandaids or, as political activist and academic Angela Davis puts it, 'difference that is not allowed to do its work. Difference that does not make a difference'.

A better resolution would be to undertake a thorough analysis of how the institution may better distribute power, followed by putting an equity and inclusion strategy in place to begin the work of being intersectional by redefining and redesigning what the institution is and who it serves.

If our institutions were intersectional, they would not only provide more seats at the table for a broader range of people and experiences, but would try to understand how the table should be redesigned for everyone to contribute and engage in future building.

If our institutions were intersectional, they would move past tokenistic consultation processes and invest in broader, more courageous, reciprocal relationships with communities most affected by historical marginalisation.

If our institutions were intersectional, they would ask themselves how the politics of race, gender, sexuality, disability and class show up in their organisations, and what role they intend to play in dismantling these barriers to access (and how much power they intend to give up in the process).

If our institutions were intersectional, they would be better positioned to secure the growing future of our creative economies as urban demographics continue to evolve.

These changing demographics are the current and future realities of the Australian cultural landscape. Our industry will either adopt an intersectional framework for engagement that will invite these communities to participate authentically as leaders and stakeholders, or it will continue to perpetuate structural and institutional practices that prioritise the 'mythical normal', resulting in the same disenfranchisement we experience today.

....

Things to keep in mind

* Intersectionality is a framework that can be used to identify structural inequalities. These inequities can be addressed through an investigation of power and equity.
* Diversity without the acknowledgment of inequity is useless. In gaining an understanding of inequity, it is vital we heal the harm and rectify the imbalance.
* Get a clear understanding of the basics of identity politics. Meet people. Ask questions. Listen. Read. Understand when it is necessary for you to lead and when it is necessary for you to follow.
* Stay checked into the work that you are doing. Be furiously vigilant about your relationships with the communities you are working with.
* Stay checked into your motivations. Gangulu activist Dr Lilla Watson credits Aboriginal activist groups in Queensland in the 1970s with the famous quote: 'If you have come here to help me, you are wasting your time. But if you have come because your liberation is bound up with mine, then let us work together'.
* Don't forget, context matters.

....

Ethics and self-determination

Tania Cañas

Ethics represents an expected standard between acceptable and unacceptable behaviour. This expected standard or 'norm/s of conduct' is often framed, understood, articulated and applied within a particular Western value-system and philosophy, reflecting a dominant mode of thinking about and understanding of the world and its relations. In this way, ethics becomes understood and applied as a singular, unmoving, universal lens.

Not challenging these assumptions might indicate that a given practice is 'doing good' or is 'well intentioned', without thinking about the impact of our own purpose and privilege within a process. Ethics becomes about the individualised and universal rather than the collective or relational.

Creative practice enables the possibility of disrupting rather than repeating modes of being. This opens up ethics, disconnects it from inherent assumptions, and has the potential to allow it to respond to each shifting moment.

Ethics as relational, ethics as movement

Ethics has often been associated with ideas of morality and character (understandings of good/bad or right/wrong). This universalisation of ethics supposes a 'right way'. This supposition can be defensive, divisive and ultimately supportive of existing power dynamics (such as using the 'good people with good intentions' excuse to justify harmful approaches under the guise of helping).

But this binary approach ignores many forms of ethics, let alone ethics that move from moment to moment, context to context and project to project. Steering away from one-size-fits-all ethics can avoid such harmful 'helping'.

A unique perspective can be found in the idea of 'relational ethics' that comes from community and liberation psychology. As Canadian nursing professor Wendy J Austin writes: 'Acting ethically involves more than resolving ethical dilemmas through good moral reasoning; it demands attentiveness and responsiveness to our commitments to one another, to the earth, and to all living things'.

The relational approach positions ethics not as something to 'have' but as something to be explored within the context of power dynamics. It asks how a project has come to exist, not just the ethics of a project itself. Relational ethics is a holistic approach. It shows how everyone is involved in a project and its context. It looks at socio-positionality, privilege and power. In a practical way, it treats ethics as something that's constantly changing, something that requires ongoing reflection and response.

American professor of philosophy Linda Martín Alcoff identifies three essential elements for taking a relational ethics approach:

- Power: what are the dynamics, organisational structure, roles?
- Locality: what social or political position do you occupy? How does this change across context, time and in relation to others?

- Discourse: where does it sit in knowledge systems and representations? What are the terms? According to what histories?

Relational ethics also invites us to ask questions about voice, autonomy and allyship:

- What are the conditions of the exchange?
- How has it come to exist?
- What is assumed?
- What values does it prioritise?
- How am I implicated in this process?
- How am I expecting others to be implicated in this process?

Ethics isn't just something to have on an individual level, and then apply to a project or community partnership. Rather, a creative project is an opportunity to interrogate, interrupt, disrupt and reconsider existing norms and modes of thinking. A useful way to interrogate ethics is to understand what it means in relation to voice, autonomy and self-determination.

Self-determination is not the same as self-expression

One cannot speak about self-determination in the context of so-called Australia without situating it within historical and ongoing First People's liberation movements.

This chapter hopes to provide an initial framework for self-determination in the context of creative practice and working with communities. However, I encourage you to engage directly with literature authored by First

Peoples to more deeply understand the practical realities of self-determination across grass-roots community organising, Blak activism, resistance and movements (such as Dr Eugenia Flynn, Professor Chelsea Watago, Dr Amy McQuire, Professor Gary Foley and the Lowitja Institute).

Just because a community is visible (or even as hyper-visible as refugees) doesn't automatically mean they have equal representation or power. Existence in a space also doesn't mean we've had autonomy by which that existence has occurred. Speech is not always autonomous. Self-expression is not the same as self-determination.

We are not just talking about who can speak, but about how speaking occurs and under what conditions. The concern is not invisibility or hyper-visibility, but rather how these visibilities have been defined by others.

Kenyan writer and academic Ngũgĩ wa Thiong'o offers a powerful definition of self-determination as 'the ever-continuing struggle to seize back their creative initiative in history through a real control of all the means of communal self-definition in time and space'. He suggests that self-determination can be understood in the collective sense, as a process, movement or 'continuing struggle'. This struggle is between that of existence and non-existence, subject and author, storyteller and story-maker, causes and consequences.

For me, this struggle was the difference between connecting to the personal, as opposed to the systemic and structural. For me, it was the difference between the label 'refugee' and that of contextual refugeeness.

**Self-expression versus self-determination:
A quick guide**

Self-expression	Self-determination
Designates spaces	Creates spaces
Offers a platform	Generates platforms
Autonomy within pre-existing parameters/categories/frames	Autonomy outside of pre-existing parameters/ categories/frames
Engages community as traditional, ethnic, identity, art form and aesthetic	Engages community as thinkers, intellectuals, politicised, critical makers
Concerned with what is visible, staged and overt	Concerned with what is not visible, staged and covert
Requires predetermined specific participation	Requires dialogical participation
Seeks community	Seeks community-led approaches
First Peoples and People of Colour voices are hyper-visible, offered to only the most visible positions	First Peoples and People of Colour voices not restricted to only the most visible
Linear process. Clear parameters, straightforward engagement, product orientated	Non-linear process. Open to create new parameters, messy, process orientated
Singular and momentary	Collective, ongoing, structural considerations
Reflective	Reflexive

The role of the researcher

Researchers, artist researchers and academics need to approach ethics in particular ways.

- Have an early conversation about the role of the researcher and define expectations. Often the role of the researcher is assumed (including by the researcher themselves). This inevitably causes conflict and misunderstandings and escalates power dynamics.
- Research isn't just documentation and evaluation, nor does it have to look like a case study with participant interviews. Consider how the process of research itself might embody community-engaged practice and creativity. How might practice-as-research be used as methodology? How might this challenge research as institutional practice?
- Consider how research can be an opportunity to 'theorise as' rather than to 'theorise for'. How might the research process be liberating and non-oppressive?
- Have an open discussion about co-publication. How might co-publication present an opportunity for co-authorship around framing, contextualising and valuing multiple forms of knowledge? How might researcher-participant modes be challenged through co-publication? How might co-publication look different across disciplines (performance, written, etc.)?

Consent isn't static – it can be withdrawn at any part of the process. Understand and make clear the parameters of consent – what you are given consent to and what you are not, what can be used as 'data' and what cannot.

Things to keep in mind

The following tips show how to use relational ethics to support self-determination. First published on the RISE Refugee website, they specifically relate to artists from outside the refugee and asylum-seeker community who are looking to work with our community.

Written in the spirit of 'nothing about us without us', they are able to be applied to all community-engaged contexts. Think about how you can adapt them to your work with communities within which you don't have a direct, lived experience.

* Focus on the process not the product. We are not a resource to feed into your next artistic project. You may be talented at your particular craft, but do not assume that this automatically translates to an ethical, responsible and self-determining process. Understand community cultural development methodology but also understand that it is not a foolproof methodology. Who and what institutions are benefiting from the exchange?

* Critically interrogate your intention. Our struggle is not an opportunity, or our bodies a currency, by which to build your career. Rather than merely focusing on the 'other' ('Where do I find refugees?' etc.), subject your own intention to critical, reflexive analysis. What is your motivation to work with this particular subject matter? Why at this particular time?

* Realise your own privilege. What biases and intentions, even if you consider these 'good' intentions, do you carry with you? What social positionality (and power) do you bring to the space? Know how much space you take up. Know when to step back.

* Participation is not always progressive or empowering. Your project may have elements of participation, but know how this can just as easily be limiting, tokenistic and condescending. Your demands on our community sharing our stories may be just as easily disempowering. What frameworks have you already imposed on participation? What power dynamics are you reinforcing with such a framework? What relationships are you creating (for example, informant versus expert, enunciated versus enunciator)?

* Know the difference between presentation and representation.

* It is not a safe space just because you say it is. This requires long-term grass-roots work, solidarity and commitment.

* Do not expect us to be grateful. We are not your next interesting arts project. Our community is not sitting waiting for our struggle to be acknowledged by your individual consciousness or highlighted through your art practice.

* Do not reduce us to an issue. We are whole humans with various experiences, knowledge and skills. We can speak on many things. Do not reduce us to one narrative.

* Do your research. Know the solidarity work already being done. Know the nuanced differences between organisations and projects. Just because we may work with the same community doesn't mean we work in the same way.

* Art is not neutral. Our community has been politicised and any art work done with/by us is inherently political. If you wish to build with our community, know that your artistic practice cannot be neutral.

The art of collaboration

Eleanor Jackson

In an interconnected world, collaboration has become the norm rather than the exception.

We now see more artists and arts organisations working with new players for a range of outcomes. These new relationships align with the more collectivist, communal and interdependent ways of working often practised by First Peoples and other cultural groups. Collaborations may be with business, industry, community, science, technology, academia, health, activism or government, to name but a few.

But what is 'good collaboration'? How can we use the experience of collaborating to create the most interesting outcomes for those who make and delight in the arts? We can start by looking at collaboration itself as an art form, a process that is as creative as the work it seeks to produce.

What is collaboration?

At the most basic level, collaboration is two or more people or organisations working together. I bring my strengths; you bring yours. Together, we create something that is more or better than we could have produced alone.

Usually, this exchange features an agreement to collaborate. The agreement need not be formal, but

genuine collaboration often involves at least an intent
to work together in a shared framework. More subtly,
however, collaboration is also a discursive process. The
way we talk about collaboration, and the discussions we
have while collaborating, form the meaning and value
of the collaboration itself. As such, while the term is
frequently used, it is also frequently misused. We often
limit our expressions of collaboration to questions of
efficiency and expense. This makes our collaborations
more transactional than transformational.

Making complex work with many parties isn't easy.
Collaborations are often reduced to doing something in
the least amount of time for the least amount of money.
But even imperfect collaborations can offer audiences
and artists great satisfaction and new experiences.

How to get started

The following questions can help shape the initial phase
of a collaboration.

- Why would I want to collaborate? Do I want to give
  something? Or get something?
- Who am I (or my organisation)? Who do I want to
  collaborate with? What are our shared and different
  values, missions, structures, strengths, needs and
  resources?
- What do I want to do? Do I want to collaborate for
  operational, tactical, strategic or transformational
  activities? Is this a clear and realistic goal that is
  understood by all?
- Where will this collaboration take place? What
  changes practically, financially and personally if

we work together remotely, in person, co-located or otherwise?
- When will we start working together and when will we stop? Can we end a collaboration before its desired outcome? Do we have the means to manage conflict and change in the collaboration?
- How will we work together? How formal does this collaboration need to be? How strong is our track record of working together with others in the past?

These questions and their answers establish a shared vocabulary to guide dialogue of collaboration.

Arts and non-arts collaborators

There are as many ways to collaborate as there are individuals and organisations to collaborate with. Typically, these behaviours take place on a spectrum of relationships (how closely we work together) and value (how much we contribute to each other). The nature, scale, risk, resources and formality of a collaboration depend on those involved and the purpose of collaboration.

Suppose a composer and their long-time friend, a nanotechnologist, decide to work together on a Symphony to Very Little Things. Their goal is merely to have some fun. This may not require a great deal of formal paperwork or discussion. But if a state symphony orchestra and national scientific research institute want to do the same thing, then more formality and discussion will be required. One form of collaboration is not necessarily better than the other.

Key principles for collaboration

Collaboration is a form of relationship. Like all relationships, it benefits from mutual work. The work of sustaining a collaboration often involves the following three things:

- Trust. Ethical behaviour, transparent communication and truthfulness are key to good collaborations. A loose, informal collaboration may thrive with these factors, but even a formal, structured collaboration will fail without the necessary trust between parties.
- Language. The way we talk about our collaborators and collaborations is meaningful. If we see a particular community as 'needing us' because they are vulnerable and disadvantaged, can they contribute equally to the project? Are men and women, older and younger people, or those from diverse cultural backgrounds, spoken about or to in particular ways?
- Time. A lack of time to relate to the people in your collaboration can lead to considerable conflict and disappointment. All industries face pressure to demonstrate impact and efficiency. But it can be transformative to challenge the 'hurry up and produce' attitude that shapes our collective thinking and biases.

Still, if you ask the above questions, can you assume all will go well? Maybe, but maybe not. This is not because working with new or different people is a bad thing. The arts, like all sectors, works within unspoken norms and behaviours. People 'know what to do' because they have learnt what to do by being a part of the group over time. These collective behaviours and attitudes influence and shape our own.

We sometimes develop narrow ways of thinking that assume everyone experiences the world the way we do. Sectors like business, technology or health use their own languages and have their own standards of behaviour. The same can be said about the arts. All sectors and groups work in particular ways and place value on different things. Sometimes, these are subtle differences. Other times, there is a great distance between parties.

Understandably, these differences and tensions can also make collaboration challenging. It is rare that collaborations allow time for relationship-based ways of working. Time is precious and resources are scarce. Often, we start with great intentions, but fall back into habitual ways of working and thinking. We make assumptions. Later, we find ourselves dissatisfied with the process or outcome. We wish that we had not collaborated at all.

These differences make it possible to rethink the dynamics of creative participation and purpose. Collaboration asks us to reflect. We reflect on what we make, how we make it, why we make it, and for whom. Exposed to another set of organisational practices, we cannot help but see ourselves differently.

With a healthy tension between the relational, practical and transactional elements of a collaboration, we can extend ourselves and our organisations. Navigating new physical terrain requires an awareness of our surroundings. This also applies to collaborative terrain. To manage newness and difference, our brains must pay attention in different ways. That attentiveness provides a rich opportunity for creativity.

Things to keep in mind

* Be reflexive and honest about yourself and your collaborators. There is no one way to collaborate, but honesty underpins most of the good ways.
* Acknowledge power. Power comes in many forms, from the interpersonal to the organisational and beyond. We cannot always make our power relations equal, but we can go some of the way if we acknowledge power and privilege.
* Work with people you respect and trust. Build this feeling by getting to know the people (in organisations) over time. If something happens to erode that trust, prioritise rebuilding it.
* Be vulnerable. This can be the great equaliser to power imbalances. It can feel risky to come together with vulnerability and openness. Do it anyway. It offers the chance to change and grow.
* Share lessons beyond your own organisation. This is not just you learning. This is the arts sector learning as a whole. Others will be emboldened by your actions. Even your inevitable, human failures.
* Let go of complete control. Things will not always go to plan. This does not mean that they have gone wrong. When reality differs from expectations, think of this as new data. Adjust your plans accordingly.

The art of facilitation

Jade Lillie and Kate Larsen

Facilitation is the practice of working with a group to achieve a collective goal by supporting participants to devise and self-determine solutions. It differs from other forms of project management in that facilitation isn't (or shouldn't be) about teaching or telling. Rather, it can be seen as a conversation, a process or an exercise in designing outcomes based on shared and agreed ambitions and wisdom.

Whether you're facilitating a new project or strategic plan, delivering a training session, or designing something as a group, there are some fundamental ways of working that can help you create a positive experience and outcome.

Creating the context

Setting the right tone from the beginning is crucial to facilitating effective conversations and collaborations.

Everything from the choice of physical or digital space, to the way you greet or welcome people, or the information or acknowledgments you provide will impact their individual experience as well as the successes you are collectively trying to achieve.

- Space. Balance the needs of yourself as facilitator and those of the group. What do you need to be present and productive? If the only fully accessible space available is one without windows, then access should take priority over natural light. However, be sure to factor in break times for fresh air.

- Welcome. Invite people into the space in the same way you would to your home or office. Greet them at the door, say hello, show them around and offer them something to eat or drink. Not doing so can create challenges later when you are in the midst of a difficult conversation or are struggling to get people to engage.
- Access. Is everyone comfortable? Do they have enough space? Can they see everything easily? Is your information available in different formats and is there a quiet space available upon request? Always ask for people's accessibility needs in advance – it can affect the type of space you need to create.

Importantly, these ways of starting a facilitation the same way you want it to finish it are about articulating a clear and consistent approach, language and behaviours that you want to see and share – not pre-empting the project's results.

Good facilitation is flexible and responsive to change.

The role of the facilitator

Being invited to facilitate a process is a privilege. It means people are trusting you to hold space, guide them through a process and deliver your agreed outcomes.

It is also a responsibility and something facilitators need to approach with careful thought and planning – to pay respect to the process and opportunity, and to make sure there is a clear line of sight to what it is hoping to achieve – a plan that can change if and when needed.

- Scope. Understanding and refining scope is key. It is misleading and not useful to make promises you can't keep. We can achieve a number of things within a facilitated process, including team building, critical conversations about specific topics, or co-designing principles for ways of working. There is, however, usually one main thing that people want to leave with. It's your job to know what this is and chart a path to get there.
- Rapport. You'll have the easiest and most enjoyable time getting to the best results if you can build rapport with and among the group. A warm welcome is key to this, as is remembering people's names and the details they share, knowing who said what, and occasionally sharing your own stories, anecdotes or sense of humour. The relationship is the project, after all.
- Results. Even the most flawless planning, welcoming and relationship building will be undermined if you can't facilitate a safe, equitable conversation or deliver what you agreed. If things change throughout a process, pause, outline and seek agreement on how that may change the agreed outcome, too.

Understanding communication and learning styles

We all learn and communicate differently, sometimes using different styles for different situations, or switching between multiple ways on any given day. It's important

for facilitators to understand our own communication
defaults and preferences, and to make sure we
accommodate our participants' styles, too.

- If you're a visual or spatial communicator, you
  understand and learn best through pictures,
  diagrams or demonstrations.
- If you're an aural communicator, you prefer listening,
  sound or music.
- Verbal or linguistic communicators prefer words,
  reading or writing.
- Physical or kinaesthetic communicators prefer using
  their bodies in some way, such as through role-play
  or walking while talking.
- Statistical communicators prefer numbers, logic
  or systems.
- Narrative communicators prefer stories, case studies
  or real-world examples.
- If you're a social or interpersonal communicator, you
  prefer to learn or discuss things with other people.
- Solitary or intrapersonal communicators prefer to
  learn or think things through on their own.

Whether online or in person, in writing or real-time,
it is vital to consider and meet the needs of any group.
Just because we think we're communicating effectively
through an aural presentation, for example, doesn't mean
that information is being received by those who prefer
written communication or need time on their own to
process what's being said.

Sharing information in different ways and
incorporating a range of different activities into your
agenda can help meet a group's diverse preferences

Communication and learning styles by Bec Sheedy

and needs. This could include personal writing tasks, pair or group activities in alternate spaces so people can move, data-led stories or anecdotes, providing handouts for people to write on or read along, or reading aloud while people quietly listen before being asked to respond.

Physical, cultural and psychological safety

As facilitators, we can never truly understand the lived experience of everyone entering a space over which we're responsible. We can be sure, however, that those experiences will be diverse, complex and intersectional, and encompass wisdom, joy, trauma and courage.

The art of successful facilitation is deeply rooted in creating the safest, most productive and generative space possible. Our role as facilitators is to make sure everyone can participate fully and equally. This includes asking ourselves questions:

- Physical safety. How accessible is the physical or digital space you're using? Is everyone able to enter and move freely around the space? Is it free of hazards? Have you provided different ways for people to get comfortable (sitting, standing, lying down)? Are people able to socially distance themselves from one another?
- Cultural safety. Is the space welcoming for First Nations people, People of Colour, disabled people? Are we the best person to facilitate a conversation? If not, should we bring on collaborators/co-facilitators or pass the opportunity on to somebody else? Does the structure or agenda of the day unconsciously privilege some people over others?

- Psychological safety. Will the facilitation start with an agreed set of behaviours and expectations? Do you have a safe word or process in place to respectfully defuse heated situations? Have you thought about how to navigate the ways that psychological safety can interact with cultural safety, such as making a collective decision to preference those with lived experience?

Creating and maintaining a physically, culturally and psychologically safe space includes respecting each other and calling out 'unsafe' or 'inappropriate' behaviours as soon as they happen. Depending on the group, you may like to design the ways of working at the beginning of the facilitation process together, with a focus on creating the safest possible space for everyone involved.

Occasionally, it may be your job to close a conversation, remove someone from the room or acknowledge unsafe behaviours. Rapport is vital in these instances, as is being prepared to have difficult conversations, even if they can sometimes have personal, professional or even financial fall-out.

....

Things to keep in mind

* Remember your context. Facilitation may be about getting the most out of other people, but facilitators still bring our own experiences and intersections into our facilitations, with the accompanying privilege and power. We need to reflect on how these may affect our processes and outcomes, and when it's appropriate to acknowledge them to the group.

* Stay in your lane. As a facilitator, you're allowed to have an opinion but should resist sharing it unless it's useful to the conversation. Make sure you share any experiences briefly and ask a follow-up question to ensure the conversation returns to the group.

* Embed equity. Ensure everyone has a chance to have their say. Ask the more active members of the group to allow space for others. Call on quieter participants or provide a range of ways for them to contribute.

* Practise. The more experience you have with facilitation, the more confident you will become. Ask to observe different people's facilitation styles, take a short course, co-facilitate with someone you admire, or offer to facilitate small group conversations pro bono to build your skills and confidence.

* Build your toolkit. Create a toolkit of facilitation activities and approaches that work for you and that accommodate different learning and communication styles. Share with other new, emerging and established facilitators. Learn from each other.

* Act quickly when things go wrong. Difficult situations often get more complicated with distance and time, so it's best to address them as quickly as possible. Acknowledge and respect what people are feeling.

Ask and listen. Reframe the conversation by asking participants to sit with their discomfort, consider the issue without taking it personally, and centre the experience of those closest to the issue. Take a break if necessary. Try to stay calm and focused on the issue and what you need to achieve. If all else fails, go back to the initial brief, the purpose for coming together and bring everyone back to the 'work' at hand.

* Follow up. Be sure to check in post facilitation. Was it everything they hoped? Was there anything you could do differently next time? It is important to close the loop.

Creating communities

Samuel Kanaan-Oringo
and Rosie Dennis

When individuals come together to create, the communities that form become a space for people to celebrate the journey that brought them together.

Engaging, collaborating and working with communities can lead to unexpected or unimaginable experiences. But what does it mean to create a new community around a project, moment or idea? And how do we make that happen?

The first time

Be prepared. Explore how you express yourself. Be ready to talk about your project or idea to potential collaborators. Work out who you want to involve. Start by talking to friends and people you already know. Grow your network and land crucial first encounters. Learn from every experience that comes your way.

If meeting people in their home, it's important to remember that you will leave the meeting knowing a lot more about them as individuals than they will know about you. These meetings are snapshots of their personal lives and will surround you with their everyday. You will meet their family through photos on the wall, and get a sense of their socio-economic background from their furnishings or the food that is served. It's important to remain open and respectful of this intimate beginning. Ask questions. Listen to their answers. Adjust your verbal and body language and your energy to make people feel comfortable.

Use these conversations to gather information and research, but also to let the person know that you are open, that you respect them and that they can trust you. Respect for their privacy is critical and permission needs to be granted before other artists or people connected to the project enter their domestic/private space.

We're in it together

As the leader of a community-engaged project, you will straddle many roles – from the overall vision to on-the-ground community engagement. It's time-consuming and unglamorous but deeply rewarding.

The process is cyclical. The community engagement fuels the artistic vision, which provokes questions and curiosity, which feeds the creative process.

Conversation is key and listening is the greatest skill you can have on the ground. An atmosphere of mutual respect fosters the freedom to 'think big' and allows discussions to lead to new insights. Encouraging contribution is for the benefit of the community and not just any one individual within it.

It's different each time, depending on the community, the place and the outcome. Knowing when to shift gears is critical – a combination of experience and intuition. At its best, this results in a combination of voices and ideas with a shared sense of ownership by the community, the artists and the audience.

Trust your own process

Here are some things to keep in mind throughout
the creating process:

- Flexibility. Prepare for impromptu art to happen.
  In the process of creating, you could be led to
  unexpected places (real or imagined) and may find
  something authentic to the work to incorporate into
  it. Make an initial plan and then allow it the freedom
  to create and recreate itself.
- Ego. As a facilitator, you need to be nimble, prepared
  to recalibrate and let go of ideas as the project evolves
  with the community's voice.
- Quality. Regardless of how you work, quality is
  found in your process and message as well as in your
  outcome. Deepen your understanding of what you're
  trying to do. Seek out modes of creation that resonate
  with your message.
- Quantity. Creating does not require you to know
  what the final product will be. Focus on producing,
  gathering and inviting material to play with and
  understand before regarding or disregarding its
  relevance or relationship to the final work.
- Community. Open dialogue and a willingness to work
  together to achieve agreed aims are vital when these
  processes are used to create collaborative work with
  a community.
- Contract. Acknowledge that this is a job for you,
  and getting a project to the finish line is you and
  your team's responsibility. This is what facilitators
  are trained to do and the community trusts their skill

and expertise to bring it all together. It's the final part of the contract.

At the start of every project, I'm already breaking up

Negotiating 'what's next' is part of your professional responsibility when working with communities – particularly communities with high levels of social disadvantage. This is regardless of what comes next, which could be the end of the project, the final performance, starting another stage, or handing it over to the community.

When forming a project, a contract exists among the people involved. This figurative contract usually lays a basis for gathering and holds the intention of what you want the project to achieve. The contract is what unites the community of individuals; it is the drum that synchronises all contributors to the beat of the same message; it is the rudder that directs the community's ambitions into a tangible goal. The contract also demands a certain level of professionalism. The collaboration is a means to an end. So it's important to outline that the project is temporary and will come to an end. Don't assume everyone understands what this means.

From the perspective of a collaborator within a community, the break-up at the end of the project is often difficult. As a professional, there is an understanding of the highs and lows of an artistic process, particularly one that culminates in a live performance or presentation. However, as a community member who may not have experienced a devised creative process before, there's likely to be a larger gap, as their 'normal' routine will have been disrupted.

Throughout the creative process, it's important to talk about what will happen when the project is over or leaves town. Find new ways to explain this throughout the process, where you can offer introductions and connections.

Things to keep in mind

* Never assume people are on the same page as you.
* Create a space where everyone is able to share their thoughts.
* Be ready to listen and serve.
* Communicate changes to the project clearly.
* Be consistent.
* If a first meeting is happening in someone's home or community space, bring food or something to share.
* If you say you'll call on a particular day and time, call on that day at that time, or let them know you need to make an alternative arrangement.
* Begin each meeting with a brief on the intentions of the gathering.
* Be mindful and respectful of the cultures represented in both the project and community involved.
* Remain open to ideas that are not fully understood.
* If you don't know something, ask.

Disability access and inclusion

Caroline Bowditch

As a society (and an arts industry in particular), there is generally great interest and enthusiasm towards access and inclusion. But what isn't always evident is how this translates into great delivery in practice. Instead, what is often done is based on 'the way we've always done it' or 'what we thought people would want'.

By not being accessible and inclusive, the 20 per cent of the population made up by disabled people are being discriminated against and excluded – plus their families, friends and associates (potentially at least 60 per cent of the population combined). Does this make good business sense?

Ableism: Power and privilege

Ableism is the oppression of disabled people. It can be systemic and/or individual, direct and indirect, intentional and unintentional. It is a term used to describe the prejudice and discrimination experienced by disabled people directly or indirectly.

Disability has been and always will be present as long as humans exist. Disability does not discriminate. It doesn't care about your gender, the colour of your skin, where you come from, where you were born or what language you speak, your socio-economic background, your sexual orientation or your gender identity. Disability is likely to come to everyone at some point in our lives. However, as a society, we still seem to view disability as something that happens to other people, or as the worst thing that could happen to anyone, something best avoided if possible.

Disabled people have always been thought of as lesser beings – viewed as leaners not lifters, takers not givers, as a drain on society, as a problem needing to be dealt with. They have been treated without dignity, forcibly incarcerated in institutions, denied human rights, been deemed as unfit parents, been denied reproductive rights and forced into poverty and isolation by systemic discrimination.

All of these assumptions, misconceptions and discriminating factors are the waters that disabled people swim in and have to negotiate on a daily basis. It is these sorts of factors that taint society's view of disabled people and generate ableist attitudes. It is these sorts of attitudes that mean everyone misses out.

As American disability activist Judith Heumann asked, 'If I have to feel thankful about an accessible bathroom, when am I ever gonna be equal in the community?'

Creative opportunity and innovation

Disabled artists are some of the most lateral, creative thinkers and problem solvers you will ever have the privilege to work with. Why? Because they constantly need to find solutions to situations or environments that aren't welcoming or accessible.

Social model thinking

According to the United Nations Convention on the Rights of Persons with Disabilities, disability is an evolving concept that 'results from the interaction between persons with impairments and attitudinal and environmental barriers that hinder their full and effective participation in society on an equal basis with others'. One way to attempt to begin to address this imbalance is by practising social model thinking.

The social model of disability is a philosophy, or way of thinking, that recognises that people are disabled by barriers created by society, not by their condition or impairment. These barriers can be found in the environment, communication or attitudes, and can have an impact on access to information, education, employment, appropriate housing or accommodation or socialisation. The consequences of these barriers can include poverty, marginalisation, discrimination and shame.

Those who subscribe to social model thinking prefer to use the term 'disabled people'. It acknowledges that we are disabled by society or the environment and not by our bodies or minds. Disability is part of our identity and culture. It connects us to a community, allows us to reclaim collective power and build disability pride.

Not viewing access and inclusion as a priority has built inequality towards disabled people into our society. But achieving inclusion is not our responsibility alone. We all have a responsibility and a role to play.

Accessible and inclusive arts have become some of the most vibrant and dynamic areas of contemporary arts practice. Sadly, this is a space rarely sought out by non-disabled artists.

Access is still considered to be a choice. Something optional often addressed at the end of a project – if there's any money left in the budget. Many companies and artists think of it as an obligation rather than as a juicy creative opportunity to create innovative or groundbreaking work.

If we, as artists and arts organisations, are in receipt of public funds, we have an obligation to create access for as many people as possible, not just a select group. We need to move away from seeing access as a drain on resources, time and quality, and see it as the most exciting creative opportunity we have available.

Creating accessible spaces: Tangible and ephemeral

At the moment, many disabled people's experience of the arts is incredibly limited. Disabled people regularly experience limited choices and a lack of autonomy. This is due to the lack of consumer consultation, information, knowledge and experience on the part of decision-makers.

There is often a lack of awareness of the invisible messages and markers that indicate to disabled people: 'You're not really welcome here'. This includes things like wheelchair access being through a back door or a convoluted route that requires an escort; by there being only one Auslan-interpreted and one audio-described show throughout a four-week run; by a lack of access information on websites or in brochures; or the lack of representation of disabled people's experience on stage, screen or creative teams.

Asking a few simple questions can massively change the way we work, interact and be in the world, and can allow everyone in a space to feel accepted, valued and valuable.

- What do you need in order for this to be the best experience for you?
- What do we need to know before we start working together?

Reluctance to ask these questions often comes from fear that we might not be able to deliver. But it's unlikely that anyone will ask for anything unreasonable or unrealistic.

As leaders, teachers and facilitators, we need to build flexibility into our projects. It's a bit like having a contingency line in a budget. Whatever structures or systems we put in place need to have an element of flexibility, too. Achieving equity is about treating everybody differently, not treating everyone the same.

Leadership and community-led practice

Visibility and presence of disabled leaders is a key component of the change process.

Disabled leaders offer us the power of possibility. They have the potential to provide society with a regular 'reality check' and other disabled people (of any age) with role models. Expectations can rise. Myths and assumptions can be shattered.

If a community group with a specific lived experience (such as disability) is led by a facilitator with a similar shared experience, 'quick trust' can be established. This quick trust allows a facilitator to ask relevant and potentially braver questions, start further into a creative process, and possibly produce faster, stronger and more interesting outcomes.

By disabled people leading, and being present and visible in society, there is less opportunity for them to be thought of as an anthropological group needing to be 'served' or 'dealt with', but rather as people who contribute and are leaders, colleagues, friends and lovers.

By having disabled leaders at the decision-making table, access and inclusion is more likely to remain present: in our minds and on our agendas.

Case study: Universal design in dance

Universal design is the 'the design of products and environments to be usable by all people, to the greatest extent possible, without the need for specialised design'. This is the RL Mace Universal Design Institute definition, based on the work of disabled American architect, product designer, educator and consultant Ron Mace.

During his time working as a non-disabled dancer with Candoco in the UK, dancer, facilitator and academic Jürg Koch observed the company's disabled dancers having to constantly adapt techniques that didn't work effectively for the diverse bodies in the room. He set about developing a class structure that had shared concept and direction, timing, rigour and flow, and allowed everyone in the room to work in a way that worked for their body.

The technique asks everyone to work to their 100 per cent and teachers to really think about the aims of their class. What skills are they trying to pass on? What is the purpose of a movement they're teaching?

Learners have to think and connect with their physicality rather than just trying to copy the body at the front of the room. But the most important thing about this practice is that it allows everyone to participate – regardless of training, style, experience or physicality.

······································

Things to keep in mind

* Be clear of the aim of your exercise, activity or session. Be open to the multiple ways that people can achieve the aim in a way that works for them.
* Invite everyone in the group to let you know what they need from you in order to have the best and most accessible experience possible.
* Offer concepts, description and demonstration in order to allow learners to access your exercise in a way that works for them.
* Ask 'need to know' not 'want to know' questions. A person's disability label is much less relevant or informative than their access requirements.
* Expect greatness of all participants. Don't be scared to correct or encourage more from disabled participants. The only way people can improve is through constructive feedback.
* Be patient, be curious and be open to learning from the bodies in the room.
* Trust yourself. Remember to breathe.
* Remember, achieving equity and inclusion is about treating everybody differently, not treating everybody the same.

······································

Bridging Deaf and hearing worlds

Claire Bridge and Chelle Destefano

Creative collaborations between d/Deaf and hearing people can lead to exciting and innovative outcomes.

Historically, d/Deaf people have often been left out when it comes to meaningful participation in the arts. We have been overlooked as creative contributors and leaders. Although things are changing, many arts professionals, organisations, artists and groups are yet to work directly with d/Deaf individuals or members of d/Deaf Communities.

Inclusion is not just about temporarily removing barriers; it's about building relationships and creating space for d/Deaf voices and perspectives. It requires a commitment to connecting and bridging the divide. Inclusion is a practice. As award-winning Deaf filmmaker, theatre creator and creative producer Sam Martin says, it requires us to 'make time to get to know each other'.

Access is a bridge. Inclusion is a relationship.

Deaf identity and deaf culture

The capital 'D' in 'Deaf' refers to those of us who identify as part of the Deaf community. We share a common culture and primarily use sign language to communicate.

In Australia, the majority of signing Deaf people use Auslan.

On the other hand, the lowercase 'd' for 'deaf' refers to individuals with varying degrees of hearing loss who may not identify with Deaf culture and may rely on speech, lip-reading, written text and hearing aids. The term 'd/Deaf' is used to encompass both groups.

People who are d/Deaf may have different preferences for how they identify, so it's important to ask and use the terminology each person prefers, such as Deaf, deaf or HoH (hard-of-hearing). We may also prefer different modes of communication depending on the situation. For example, a bilingual Deaf person who uses both English and Auslan might choose to speak and lip-read in quiet, one-on-one social settings with a hearing person who doesn't use Auslan, and require an Auslan interpreter and note-taker in meetings or busy work environments. Interpreters are usually required in circumstances where others are not fluent in sign language or information is not provided in accessible ways.

'Deaf Gain', 'Deaf Pride' and 'Deafhood' are central concepts in Deaf culture and identity. 'Deaf Gain' emphasises that being Deaf is not a disability or a loss, but a source of unique experiences, perspectives and strengths. It highlights Deaf people's value and our contribution to society. 'Deafhood', coined by Deaf academic and activist Dr Paddy Ladd, refers to how we develop and embrace a positive Deaf identity that focuses on possibilities rather than limitations. 'Deaf Pride' represents our sense of identity and community and offers a term of resistance in a hearing-dominated world.

Art is an important way for Deaf people to express ourselves and share our unique perspectives. Deaf-led art may explore our culture, humour, language or creativity. It may help people understand and appreciate our identity, create a sense of belonging, or challenge unfair systems. Through Deaf-led art, Deaf role models can lead the way and make a difference to how d/Deaf people are perceived.

What allies can do

Allies can participate in decolonising deafness by standing up against oppression and unfair power structures that marginalise and silence d/Deaf people. We want to disrupt these unfair systems and take back our power.

- Make sure d/Deaf voices and experiences are heard and respected.
- Advocate for our rights, and ensure we are treated fairly and have the same opportunities as everyone else.
- Take care of our d/Deaf communities and create environments where we can thrive. Nurture d/Deaf ecologies.
- Employ us in your organisations.
- Celebrate our language and use it proudly.

Intersectional identities

Acknowledging our diverse, intersectional identities values our individuality and differences, and guards against stereotypes and over-generalisations.

Aesthetic access

Aesthetic access considers content and materials in ways that include everyone, including d/Deaf people. We want to make sure that access is not an afterthought, but something that is incorporated right from the start.

- Include d/Deaf people, a Deaf consultant and Auslan interpreters in the planning and design of your project.
- Design spaces where d/Deaf people can easily see everything. Use colours that stand out and don't blend with the background. Avoid backlighting that can make it hard to see. Be conscious of strong changes in lighting, which require time to visually adjust. Make sure interpreters are clearly visible. Reserve seating for Deaf audiences for a clear view.
- Embed access in design. Include an audio describer or interpreter as a character in the performance, incorporate captions in the set design, present sound elements in a visual way, or include links to accessible materials, such as a QR code link to an Auslan video translation of text.
- Explore different ways to express meaning through touch, smell, visuals and movement.
- Be aware of visual fatigue. Visual concentration can be tiring. Build in rest breaks or moments of visual quiet so d/Deaf collaborators and audiences can take a break and reset.

Being inclusive requires thinking about intersecting aspects of d/Deaf identity, such as Aboriginality, gender, religion, sexuality, ethnicity, nationality, class, occupation, education, mental health and disability.

For example, someone may be Deaf/Blind or identify as First Nations/Deaf/LGBTQIA+ or be a woman who is both Deaf and Muslim. These intersections of identity can expose d/Deaf people to compounded discrimination.

Making time to get to know each other and asking us what we need can help to create a safe and inclusive working environment.

Audism, power dynamics and precarity

Audism is a form of discrimination and prejudice against d/Deaf individuals. It assumes that hearing and using speech is superior, while being d/Deaf or hard of hearing is inferior. It privileges hearing and speaking as the norm and looks at deafness as a deficit.

Examples of audism include: expecting d/Deaf people to lip-read; not giving a deaf child the chance to learn sign language; banning d/Deaf people from using sign language; only providing information in spoken or written English; hearing people talking over us or not pausing to allow us to contribute in a meeting; excluding us because of access costs.

Audism can cause unequal power dynamics to arise in collaborations between d/Deaf and hearing people, with hearing individuals often holding more power and control. This can lead to d/Deaf people feeling marginalised or disempowered.

Uncertainty around access provision can have a significant impact on d/Deaf people, create delays, promote mistrust and compound stress. For example, not knowing if an interpreter has been booked can lead to miscommunication and difficulties participating or building relationships. Ask Deaf people to nominate their preferred interpreters or booking agency. Organising interpreters, note-takers or captioning services in advance shows that you value accessibility.

Give d/Deaf collaborators space and agency. We have valuable perspectives and contributions to offer. Recognise and appreciate our strengths. Be open to our ideas and feedback. By being mindful of power imbalances, we can build more equal partnerships and better communication.

Cultural appropriation and tokenism

When a hearing person uses sign language without proper training or cultural understanding, it can be seen as appropriation. Cultural appropriation is extractive, disrespectful and perpetuates systems of oppression and colonisation of d/Deaf people. Elevate Deaf people and preference working with Deaf signers, teachers, artists, or consultants.

Similarly, inviting d/Deaf people to participate, but not providing us with equal opportunities to contribute or make decisions, could be seen as box-ticking. Tokenism is evident if nothing changes or improves after you work with us.

And don't forget to connect with d/Deaf groups and organisations to let us know about and promote your accessible event. 'Having an interpreter is brilliant, but if there are no Deaf people there, and we don't know about your event, then there are no real mutual benefits,' Martin says.

Things to keep in mind

* Set aside a realistic budget for access and inclusion.
* Ask people how they prefer to communicate and what access they need. This includes discussing their preferred language, such as Auslan, and any assistive technologies they may use, such as speech-to-text apps, pen and paper, or video calls with captioning.
* Use clear and simple communication. Avoid complex sentences or confusing jargon. Be patient. Allow time for questions and clarification.
* Check in regularly to see how things are going and ask for ways to improve. It's important to expect there may be misunderstandings along the way.
* When speaking to d/Deaf people, face the person directly and speak clearly and naturally. Avoid making exaggerated facial expressions or covering your mouth.
* Look at us as you speak, not our interpreters.
* Visual aids, diagrams and images can be helpful. Make sure to pause and give us time to look at them.
* Provide a visual rating of the show's audio content (for example, a 100 per cent visual rating might describe an exhibition without sound, music or dialogue and a 50 per cent visual rating could describe an event with a subtitled spoken introduction).
* Record a digital online version of your event. Interpreters are often only booked for one-off performance dates. An online version allows d/Deaf people to access the event at other dates and times, and can include both interpreting and captioning as needed.

* Learn about Deaf culture by asking questions or participating in a Deaf awareness workshop that is designed and facilitated by Deaf people. Consider enrolling in Auslan classes or finding a Deaf tutor. Learn how to fingerspell the alphabet.

* Recognise and value the contributions of d/Deaf artists and collaborators by paying us for our work.

* Most importantly, as Deaf multidisciplinary artist and Auslan cultural and accessibility consultant Danni Wright says, 'Be open and flexible'.

••

Labels: From avoidance to acceptance

Jeremy Smith

We have all left an event or a conference at some point still wearing a name tag around our necks or physically adhered to ourselves via a sticky label. We forget about it until someone points it out, or we see it in the reflection of a mirror. Then we giggle with embarrassment, perhaps roll our eyes and feel like a bit of a dork. Then we take off the label and put it in the bin.

We put the label in the bin because we can. It's only temporary and has served its purpose. It told people our name, perhaps our pronouns, maybe where we work. But we are so much more than those few things.

Whether we acknowledge or even understand it, each of us has intersectional aspects to our identities. Each of these exposes us – consciously or subconsciously – to discrimination and privilege, advantage and disadvantage, marginalisation and inclusion. We are never one thing at one time – and we accept or inherit different aspects of our character at different moments.

So much of what builds this lived experience transcends labels. Yes, definitions are useful and important at the right moments – but every person we encounter brings with them varied lived experiences of the 'life behind the label' that means we cannot so easily be defined.

Self-determination takes time

Young people, refugees, regional, disabled, disadvantaged, CALD (culturally and linguistically diverse), Indigenous, at-risk ... you name it, there's a label for it. But why? Whose label is it anyway?

My position and thoughts on 'labels' are informed by my own lived experience. I am a gay, Caucasian middle-aged man with grey-green eyes, brown hair, and a short beard with some greyness around the chin. I also have achondroplasia, which is the most common form of dwarfism. I was born with the condition in the mid-1970s– a time when the medical model of disability reigned supreme.

As a family, we never openly spoke about my 'diagnosis'. I think my parents thought of labels as something to fear – an unnecessary burden that would make it harder to push back against the medical 'experts' and attitudes of the time.

The 'treat him normal and he'll be right' approach prevailed. So, the 'disabled' label was never chosen by myself, my family or those close to me. But that didn't stop dozens of others doing so on my behalf and labelling me as a 'person with a disability' through my childhood, teens, 20s and 30s – without my permission, without my consent and without my input.

My high school told my parents I should be enrolled at a school for disabled students. My university questioned my ability to climb a ladder and to rig lights (until I demonstrated to them that I could). And in my professional career, I have been co-opted and coerced onto a range of equity, diversity, access and/or inclusion working groups, labelled without my consent, and included as a statistic on organisational diversity and demographic data.

It was at the ripe old age of 39 that I finally chose to fully embrace my difference and identify as a 'disabled person'. I was invited to be part of a participatory, immersive storytelling project that asked me to think and talk about what it was like to be me. It allowed me to reflect on how I had been treated, and realise that I was hiding part of who I am – to be easy, convenient or undisruptive, to avoid being a problem or to just get on with things.

I realised I needed to accept and embrace being disabled. Avoiding or erasing that would continue to impact my life and quality of living in negative ways. I made a self-determined choice, at the right time. I don't see disability or being disabled as a label I want to avoid any longer – it's intrinsic to who I am and how I see things. It is part of who I am and I'm proud of it – disabled and gay.

The dangers of mis-labelling

When we mislabel an individual or a community, so much can quickly unravel. So much can be damaged. Engagement can erode through lost faith and lost trust. People can be hurt and offended. Relationships that take years to develop can be broken by a poorly chosen word.

Sometimes, labels are important and necessary. People who proudly and loudly adopt a certain label often do so to create disruption and to agitate for change (though sadly, they can then sometimes be portrayed as difficult by those with fear or guilt).

Otherwise, labels are reductive, especially when imposed by others without consent. History tells us labels can frequently be about oppression and deficit – a means for those with power to 'other' and 'marginalise'. The whole premise of diversity and difference in our industry and broader society is one that is fraught with an abundance of siloes and categories.

Even now that I am openly and proudly disabled, people still mislabel me. I am not a person 'with a disability' – disability is not a handbag, nor is it a pet dog that I can choose to have 'with' me whenever I choose. I am disabled by society, by actions, by the attitudes of others, and by a system that is unable to fully adapt to or include me.

Structural and systemic change isn't possible without calling out certain shortfalls or biases around employment, participation and inclusion. Dedicated initiatives, opportunities and interventions for communities, individuals or groups of people with a shared lived experience are critical steps towards equity and justice in our industry. But these cannot be imposed – they need to be developed through deep listening, consultation and agreement.

The learning behind the labels

History confirms that the politics of identity and community groups have manifested in different languages and labels over time. Many of these terms are now old-fashioned or problematic, but often go unquestioned or are used without knowing the background behind them.

In the disability space, for example, labels too often

follow what's known as the medical model of disability. This means individuals are labelled by their conditions or impairments, which makes them appear as lesser or someone in need.

The social model of disability uses the label 'disabled people' instead to acknowledge that people are disabled by their environment.

UK activist and educator Nim Ralph gives another alternative with the radical model of disability, which recognises that 'the social construction of disability was manifested by groups with power with the aim of maintaining that power – economically and politically – by actively marginalising sections of society'.

As Toronto-based disabled, queer and trans anti-poverty activist AJ Withers writes, 'Radical disability activists acknowledge that we do not control the definition of disability – that it is defined by those with power to their benefit'.

Labels are great in your pantry – for your Tupperware containers and spice rack – but think deeply about why you would use them on a person or community. Always remember, it is important to ask a person or community what labels are meaningful to them.

We are human – more than just words. It's up to each of us to show respect and care through making an effort to self-educate and to not assume we know the 'right' thing to say or do. We need to 'turn up' and 'speak up' when we see power imbalances, such as someone being mislabelled.

We need to draw on our collective difference and learn from each other's lived experience to gain perspective and seek justice and equity in the work that we do as colleagues, allies and accomplices.

....

Things to keep in mind

∗ Motivation and intention. Before we apply a label, we should ask ourselves why we feel the need to do so. What is the endgame we're playing? Ask a person or community what labels are meaningful to them.

∗ Lived experience. Consider the person, group or community we are working with and speak about their lived experiences, individually and collectively, as a means to portray what we would otherwise attach to a label.

∗ Self-determination and consent. Have we consulted, and do we know if the person or people we are describing agrees with our word choices? Is it a description the person or people themselves have said directly to us as a way they choose to self-identify? When funding applications ask you about your 'target communities', are you using words that community would never use to talk about itself?

∗ Timing and fluidity. People's identities, perspectives and experiences shift over time. Some aspects of oneself may be permanent or temporary, acquired or circumstantial. Each day brings new lived experiences.

∗ Intersectionality. We are rarely one thing at once. Labels can be reductive, are often imposed and do not tell a full and accurate picture. Describing someone's lived experience allows the chance to explore and unearth multiple sides of their story and perspective.

∗ Systemic change. Think about moments where a label can be used for good. For instance, in recruitment, selection criteria, priorities and values. But words on paper should not automatically translate as a label on an individual. Consider the different ways people, groups or communities may meet in their own terms the words or labels we are seeking to highlight.

* Fear and power. Never forget, labels can be manufactured and imposed by those wishing to assert power and influence. They can marginalise and destabilise – and subsequently, cause fear and angst among parts of our society, which can lead to conflict and damage. Take care.

Creative lives and contemporary ageing

Tristan Meecham and Bec Reid

By 2030, one in six people in the world will be aged 60 years or over. By 2050, this age group will double from what it is now. With this significant demographic shift, how well people age is an issue of increasing priority, as is how we represent and include older people within arts and cultural practice and, indeed, our lives.

We are at a crossroads of opportunity to centralise art making and creativity within contemporary ageing: for making space for clear, unapologetic and purpose-driven creative actions for and with older people, for valuing the contributions of varied lived experiences, and for recognising older people as universities of invaluable intergenerational expertise. They are the source.

Ageing is intersectional

Age is not a community, but rather a collection of individuals experiencing spectrums of joy, love, connection, trauma and isolation – all with very specific needs and varying capacities.

Older people from under-represented or marginalised communities can experience additional issues. For example, older LGBTQIA+ Australians have lived through a time when being LGBTQIA+ could result in imprisonment, enforced medical 'cures',

Ageing vs ageism

Ageing is universal but ageism (or discrimination against someone because of their age) in Western culture is rife. The lack of visible, diverse stories about ageing well contributes to the cultural and social stigma surrounding older people.

The ongoing, multiplied impacts of social isolation and loneliness are key issues for all of us, but acutely more so for older people in a digitised, AI-facing, pandemic-affected world. There can also be an intertwining of ageism and ableism (or discrimination against someone because of their experience of disability, which increases with age), as they both assign value based on assumptions about someone's capacity or incapacity.

Western cultures aren't great at holding the experiences and wisdom of older people at their core. But this is something we can learn and improve upon. The great gift we have on these lands we call Australia is the proximity and opportunity to learn from First Nations peoples, who daily articulate and acknowledge their relationships to their lands, cultures and Elders.

First Nations Elders participate in ongoing, timeless and intergenerational solidarity by taking a holistic approach to sharing knowledge, values and culture based on deep listening – connected to and responsible for the land and each other.

loss of employment or rejection by family and friends. For many, impending older age has meant older LGBTQIA+ people are going back into the closet, for fear of being deprived of companionship or quality care when they need it most. Others require specific consideration of their social, economic and cultural experiences and circumstances.

As practitioners, we can think of our projects as 'gifts' that celebrate the varied lived experiences of collaborators, participants and audiences. Such 'gifts' could be a reciprocal relationship between an artist and community, the removal of barriers (perceived or real) to contemporary arts experiences, or a public celebration that connects diverse people or shifts time and place. Art can empower people to feel part of a bigger community, in the same way sporting events can unite different tribes.

For these reasons and more, generating swift trust with older participants is critical. Some approaches include:

- ensuring people are met at the door with a warm welcome
- asking if you can respectfully hold someone's hand or take them for a spin around the dance floor
- remembering how regular attendees take their tea
- over-catering to ensure people can have takeaway food packs
- making room for one more at the table.

Holding space in these contexts can be both complex and simple. We have learnt to:

- pay attention
- model generous, empathetic behaviour

- embrace intersectional factors and the nuances they require
- meet people where they are in the moment
- hold space to be together in creative and culturally enriching experiences
- be responsible for our own generosity.

Ageing is intergenerational

Accessing the wisdom of older people can simultaneously locate us across the past, present and future. Older people are universities that we can access and celebrate by not being patronising, by co-designing both moment-to-moment and long-game decisions and, vitally, through maintaining a sense of humour.

Engaging with older people, especially if they're at higher risk of isolation, often requires patience, fortitude, tenacity and collaboration – paying attention and building connections, one relationship, one cuppa, one dance at a time.

We've learnt to foreground access and inclusion by taking time to learn each other's rhythms, time to find common ground, and time to breathe life into the creative possibilities that are built upon trust. Once trust is flourishing, we can see and feel the creative possibilities on the horizon. It becomes energising to make creative decisions together because all parties understand the choices available to them.

When creative choices and outputs are equally satisfying for young and old, it creates a timelessness and relevance, and the possibilities of more connection points start to reveal themselves.

The role of creativity in contemporary ageing

Curiosity is ageless and creativity is universally good for us. Most of us would have witnessed the immeasurable cognitive, emotional, physical, social and/or spiritual benefits that occur when people access creative experiences. The metabolic twinkle is undeniable.

Imagine if every aged-care environment across Australia had an artist-in-residence built into its functionality with as much acceptance as any other professional in the team (like Village Landais in France). Imagine if every new public housing or infrastructure project was co-designed by children and older people to embrace intergenerational living.

Dr Mike Rungie from the Global Centre for Modern Ageing imagines what would happen if there was a price on dependency making, akin to carbon making. Just like taxing businesses for their environmental footprint, this could put a price on public health care and its economic and cultural cost – and see the prescription of social activity coming to the fore as creative experiences lower reliance on medications and save the government-of-the-day's bottom line.

So how can art makers participate in deep and dynamic systemic change in contemporary ageing? When starting a project, we invite you to consider these questions:

- Why does the idea or work need to happen?
- Who is it for? How are they involved in its design and decision-making?

- Who is going to do the work, to make it come alive with full trust? Are you genuinely the best person to lead, facilitate, champion or embody the project?
- What are the personal ingredients essential for those 'on the floor' to interface with participants/ stakeholders/audiences?
- Have you considered the historical, cultural and socio-political context of the people you are working with?
- When/how will you know it's working?
- When/how will you know it's not working?
- Who's listening / who's witnessing?
- What's your answer to 'can we do this all the time?'
- What can you offer today, tomorrow, next year?
- What does success really look like for everyone involved?

Other things to think about:

- Public awareness. How can we create offers and actions that increase the visibility of older people?
- Political bi-partisanship. How can we advocate to affect genuine cultural change for ageing well?
- Investment. How can we gain the political will and money to make contemporary ageing a reality for all, regardless of socio-economic circumstances?
- The long game. How can we support the future of contemporary ageing we want to experience ourselves?

· ·

Things to keep in mind

* Decide on the pace you're going to go at (both literally and figuratively), together.
* Say your older counterpart's name and say it aloud. Often. To them, for them, for yourselves.
* Never assume everyone in the room is hearing and understanding the same thing. There may be seen and unseen factors affecting people's capacity to absorb the information. Double and triple check. Ask and then ask again.
* Always check and recheck with folks and be prepared to listen and relisten, especially when responses can be heart-clenchingly difficult to hear.
* You can't be everything to everyone. In fact, it's usually healthier that you're not. You know what you're offering across a specific moment in time and that's where you agree to meet.
* Ask yourself what you need in order to do your best work. Then remember to ask others what they need, too.
* Enjoy the rituals you'll devise with your collaborators and counterparts. These may be quirky anthems you sing together, talismans you collectively keep, or in-jokes that you share. These are identity- and culture-making. These are often as important as the project itself.
* Remind yourself the older person you're collaborating with has almost definitely also felt the things you have felt in your life so far. First kiss, first heartbreak.

* Look out for speed bumps. Remember that the thing you never thought of will likely surprise and/or trip you up. Name it, apologise and/or acknowledge it, listen and move on.
* Take courage to recognise natural ends of project life spans, lines of enquiry or zeitgeist timescales.
* Whether you're an artist, a maker, a doer or a shaker, trust your conviction to sniff out the next place to be, the next question to ask, the next community member to connect with – and back yourself as you shape your response.

Collaborating with children and young people

Lenine Bourke

The ways we engage with children and young people is changing. New trends include the rise of artistic work for babies and toddlers and innovations in work for young children – especially preschool and early primary years, and those with diverse cultural and access needs.

A gap is emerging in terms of creative work with middle years and upper primary students. What was once a plethora of creative practice for secondary-school students (often called 'youth arts') has more recently come to include increased autonomous engagement by young people, including with digital forms.

Autonomy essentially means having the freedom to act independently. Autonomy for young people and children can be complicated not only by their age but also by other facets of their lives. All elements of this diversity need to be considered when planning for their full engagement.

Age does not make a community

Children and young people do not form a 'community' just because of their age bracket. Being a baby or a three-year-old is a vastly different experience to being an eight- or 18-year-old. Like any group of people, one identifying factor does not necessarily make a community.

Children and young people have many other life circumstances to consider: economic status, cultural backgrounds, locations, family structures, the friends or peers they have (or don't), the schools they attend, hobbies and interests, religion, gender, sexuality, disability and neurodiversity, where they like to hang out and how independent they can be. Working with children and young people who are networked into these communities provides rich possibilities for any project or collaboration.

Autonomy is not a given

Being under the age of 18 makes autonomous participation in arts and cultural activities complicated. As much as a six-year-old would like to be involved in something, if their legal guardians aren't able to access the information, or aren't committed to the interests of their children, it creates a barrier to participation and engagement. Specific circumstances around language, disability, trauma, culture, family or lifestyle differences can also provide additional challenges or considerations.

Parents may not understand the differences between formal or participatory arts classes and deeper, artist-led practices whereby children and young people are able to autonomously express themselves, their beliefs, values, stories and lives. Explaining the merits and artistic possibilities of such different experiences can be a communication challenge.

Many projects for or with children and young people give adults the decision-making power. Now more than ever, it is time to interrupt this idea and provide real decision-making opportunities for children and young people. These include budgets, venues, content, marketing, social media and governance. Not just the art, but everything.

Art asks us to be curious. You may notice changes in your young collaborators over time, as their confidence increases – not only in the art-making process but also in their ability to make more decisions for themselves. This can be a positive outcome for some families, but can cause some tension (and more barriers) in others.

Art forms need relevance

Some projects focus on artists 'teaching' a creative skill like singing, acting or painting. But developing a new skill or learning about an art form can be inhibiting when so much is new already – including the people, the content, the process and the very experience of having freedom and autonomy. And what happens if the child or young person doesn't develop that skill in the allocated time?

Community-engaged practitioners could also consider using art and cultural forms taken from life: cooking, fashion, music, walking, sport, expressive media, photography, audio, video, talking, writing, making things, parties, self-publishing, design, performing, moving, making noises, making selections of things or collecting. Using an art form that comes from your young collaborators' lives will make projects more relevant, build on the skills they already have, and make them more confident.

Participation or collaboration

Art projects for children and young people are often based on a participation framework (such as a workshop, class, lesson or six-week project) that results in participants performing or presenting learnt skills in a final showing.

Developing a framework for collaboration and creative development can provide a more flexible and relaxed approach. Rather than starting a project with a fixed idea of what will happen, a facilitated, live and co-created approach can embrace children and young people as collaborators, along with the artistic and production team. It can also consider their families or supporters as co-collaborators, as well as any other organisations, businesses, venues or volunteers engaged with the project. This is usually a very large group of people and requires a lot of energy to ensure that everyone understands what collaboration feels like and how decisions are made – putting the young people at the centre of the project and encouraging shared creative and logistical decision-making.

It is important to explain the expectations of the collaboration and for everyone to be able to explain what they think is essential to make the power dynamic between adults and young people more equal. This may involve asking the following questions:

- Who are your primary collaborators?
- Whose artistic opinions matter most?
- Who decides the way the creative work will develop?
- Where should this work take place?
- How is the form and content woven together with everyone?

Audiences or members of the general public are also part of the process. Artistic works are completed when they are experienced by an audience.

The radically flexible practitioner

What is a radically flexible practitioner (RFP)?

- Radical. They are able to do something in an extreme way.
- Flexible. They are capable of bending without breaking.
- Practitioner. They are an arts and cultural practitioner who is actively engaged professionally.

This is a skill set, a response to working across these age groups, and also a proposal for moving this practice area forward.

Because of the complexity of collaborating with children and young people, the level of flexibility required goes beyond throwing out a workshop plan when things go a little bit left field. Instead, RFPs exhibit a massive array of skills, ideas, artistic responses, experiences, opportunities and solutions to guide a group through any interruption.

In fact, an RFP embraces change and new ideas, especially those initiated by their young collaborators. They are able to respond to all of the interruptions in a project, no matter how absurd they are. This can open up amazing new creative storytelling that may end up in the final outcome.

Things to keep in mind

* Gain as much knowledge about the lives of the people you are collaborating with as possible.
* Participation, access or cultural needs may not be obvious at first, and it may not be appropriate to ask up front or have someone fill out a form. Be open to feedback and use observations to gauge signs of fatigue, hunger, thirst, anxiety or stress.
* Build positive relationships through open communication with carers, friends or trusted adults in the lives of children and young people.
* Make things free. Focus on voluntary and conceptual participation to allow access for all possible participants. Include face-to-face and online options, depending on circumstances.
* Be clear about shared intellectual property and moral rights. Talk about authorship and the ownership of ideas, and appropriately credit (with permission) all of those involved, including children and young people. Collaborative works need new models for recognising shared creativity.
* Make sure the debrief, reflection or evaluation is different from the ending of a project. An ending should be a celebration and a way for collaborators to know that part of the project is over. If people are having trouble letting go or ending their relationships, you can consider meeting up at a set date in the future. Or perhaps look for funds to continue if the quality of experience was substantial.
* Let consultation and experimentation guide the form, and encourage your collaborators to guide the content. Be encouraging of these lines blurring and

provide agency for everyone in the project to explore the nuances of form and content.

* Use tablets, phones, audio recorders, drawings, notes, books or journals to document children and young people's lives while also giving them agency to generate content. For example, using photos from events in their lives that show specific rites of passage or milestone moments not only gives insight into contemporary childhood but also into the broader diversity of each child's life.

* Children and young people want the final product to look and feel as good as possible. Remember that they are trusting you to manage this and to be their advocate in arts centres or public places.

* Volunteers play an integral role from the beginning. These can be adults working with young people, or young people working with children. They might be known to your young collaborators or begin as strangers. They may be employed by a partnering organisation, or respond to a call out for volunteers. Briefing and setting the tone and style of practice is fundamental for any project. Many volunteers might not have experienced your process and rely on school-based techniques in managing group dynamics. Educate your whole team on your processes.

* Ensure the lead facilitator is the most appropriate artist for the specific group.

* Don't forget: interruptions and changes are often opportunities for inspiration or for new concepts to emerge, and be folded back into our practices.

Working with queer communities and artists

Daniel Santangeli

There are lots of letters in LGBTQIA+ for a reason.

Queer community isn't one group. It's a quickly evolving space consisting of many interlaced communities with radically different needs, producing some of the most deeply perceptive and culturally important work.

Lesbian, gay, bisexual, trans and gender diverse, queer and questioning, intersex, asexual and allies, plus all other gender and sexuality diverse identities and intersectionalities that don't fit into neat Western and hyper-visible categories – these people are the artists and audiences of queer work. As producers and artists working in queer culture, we are operating in four fields simultaneously:

- a community-engaged space actively maintaining healthy relationships
- an intersectional space acknowledging the full diversity of queer communities
- an artistic space focused on achieving impactful arts experiences for audiences
- a human rights context.

Or put another way: in a world hostile to queer communities, your job is to support LGBTQIA+

communities to make great art in a way that builds on their strengths and leaves them feeling more enriched than when you started.

Queer excellence

Borrowing from the notion of 'black excellence', queer excellence is the belief that LGBTQIA+ people have the right to excel and have unique cultures worth celebrating.

Australia has a vibrant, fierce and burgeoning (but also fragile) queer ecology. Re-enculturation, reclamation of history, diversity, and unique contribution to art forms as a result of queer lived experiences are all hallmarks of queer excellence – but each of these hallmarks need nurturing in order to thrive.

It is rare to hear anyone talk about queer excellence. The dominant discourses in queer communities tend to be about 'pride' (think pride parades), 'community' (think 'oh, he's a member of the community'), 'equality' (think 'love is love' campaigns), 'health' (think mental health and HIV) and 'party culture' (think Mardi Gras). These discourses have changed society for the better – saved lives and forged queer communities. But there are some other important questions about queer culture(s) that are rarely asked:

- Whose stories are the most pressing, and what investment and nurturing do they need in order to be heard?
- What does our geographic reality and diasporic, postcolonial make-up mean for the kind of queer culture we hope to have in five, ten or 20 years time?

- What do our local experiences of living in diverse bodies offer as a unique perspective to the rest of the world?
- Do endless references to RuPaul's *Drag Race* and *Queer Eye* risk us becoming a totally Americanised queer culture?

Know your queer context

In post-marriage-equality Australia, many people think that we don't need queer festivals, queer cultural organisations or queer art. We do – particularly in light of growing conservatism and far-right extremism locally and internationally that is directly targeting LGBTQIA+ bodies.

Intersecting with the human-rights lineage of queer history (which itself is a non-linear, multifaceted social force that contains within it many political movements for LGBTQIA+ peoples) are deeply felt personal quests for visibility and acceptance, as well as a form of academic critique for the radical querying of society's structures. Understanding the social forces at play within your own queer context is vital to working within it and shaping it.

Creating a queer context for LGBTQIA+ artists and culture makers enables them to explore themes that don't resonate in the same way in a gender- and hetero-normative context (the belief that binary gender and heterosexuality is the norm in social, political and religious life). There is too much to say on how Western society and colonialism generated and entrenched gender- and hetero-normativity. But it is important to note that queer people are still reconciling with and undoing the forces behind it.

Providing audiences with a queer space lets them see their lived experiences in relation to others. It reinvigorates the hidden history and ideas of queer art. And it creates visibility for those elements of our queer communities who don't have a voice in mainstream society.

We need to make the world a queerer place.

Make space

Producing queer cultural experiences is about making space for queer culture. To do so, here are a series of useful questions you can ask yourself and those you're working with:

- Who is not here that should be here? This is a common question in community-engaged practice that gets to the heart of inclusivity.
- What do we need to do to make things safe? What signals safety for particular queer communities? What safety measures can you actively put in place? This could include things like all-gender bathroom signage for trans and gender-diverse communities; incorporating the black and brown stripes on the rainbow flag for queer and trans People of Colour and queer First Nations peoples; chill-out zones in party contexts; or using youth workers when engaging with young people.
- Does this need to be a Trojan horse? American community-organiser Saul Alinsky's second rule in *Rules for Radicals* is 'Never go outside of the experience of your people'. Sometimes, combining mainstream gay and lesbian audiences with art

focused on intersectionality and innovation does not mix well! Part of the challenge is in packaging a work so it is accessible to an audience without losing any of the artists' integrity.

Inclusive language

Inclusive language is an immediate sign of safety for queer people. This includes the language we use to refer to each other, particularly when it comes to talking about identity, gender and sexuality.

- Create a culture of self-education and curiosity about language. No-one likes being policed on their language, so aim for a generative culture instead. Tactics may include putting an inclusive language guide in your organisation's induction notes, actively talking about preferred language at the beginning of a creative process, arranging inclusivity training for the team you are working with, or sharing anecdotes of best practice in team meetings.
- Terminology changes. Language evolves; society changes and the words we use to describe our lived experiences change, too. Be nimble in your thinking on language. Best practice is to never impose terminology on an individual or a group. Follow their lead and use the words they want to use to describe themselves.
- People change, discover things about themselves or change how they articulate their identity. How you refer to people may change over the time that you know them.

- Get pronouns right. Pronouns are the words we use to refer to people when we are not using their name (he/him, they/them and she/her). In mainstream society, a person's pronouns are assumed based on appearance, but this can cause a lot of emotional harm for people who are trans and gender diverse. Changing a culture from assumption to respectful enquiry can be challenging. Some approaches include saying what pronouns you use when introducing yourself, adding pronouns to email signatures, and creating pronoun badges.
- It's OK to get it wrong. The challenge of language use is bigger than any individual. Don't punish individuals if they trip up. Be respectful when correcting someone on their terminology. If someone is repeatedly misgendering or using the wrong language, it could be a cultural problem within your organisation, project or industry – so also focus on changing that culture.
- Be wary. Language can be used as a weapon. Identity politics can be restricting. And both can be used as tools (sometimes unintentionally) to alienate.

Lateral violence in queer communities

Lateral violence is aggression, oppression and violence carried out between and within minority groups. While there is a perception that all LGBTQIA+ people live happily together under the rainbow, lateral violence exists between members of queer communities.

Trauma-informed practice

With its origins in community health and human services, trauma-informed practice recognises that past experiences of trauma can have an ongoing impact on an individual's agency as well as their response to crises, sense of safety, and capacity to develop trust and form relationships.

The American Centers for Disease Control and Infection (CDC) Office of Readiness and Response collaborated with the Substance Abuse and Mental Health Services Administration's National Center for Trauma-Informed Care on six guiding principles for taking a trauma-informed approach:

1   Safety
2   Trustworthiness and transparency
3   Peer support
4   Collaboration and mutuality
5   Empowerment and choice
6   Awareness of the interplay between trauma responses and an individual's culture, history, religion, education, gender and sexuality.

It's essential that community-engaged practitioners incorporate these principles into our practice to ensure we have the time, capacity, resources and expertise available to do this work well.

It's also important to note that community-engaged practitioners are often not trained counsellors or social workers – if you can't do this work in a well-resourced and supported way, it may have detrimental effects on community members.

This can include territorialism, a collision of varying agendas or perspectives, LGBTQIA+ people operating from a place of trauma, or communities directing their anger towards easy targets (rather than society's seemingly unbreachable heteronormative structures).

If you are subject to criticism or lateral violence, be prepared to engage in conversation about the issue at hand, drawing on a trauma-informed methodology. But also learn to recognise toxic relationships and establish strong boundaries to protect yourself and others.

Things to keep in mind

* Intersectionality and diversity are key. LGBTQIA+ communities are not all the same, so your artists and audiences shouldn't be either.
* Focus on queer excellence. Ask those you are working with what queer excellence looks like to them and how you can help achieve it.
* Understand your queer context. Find out what events, people, policies or social forces have shaped your queer context. Invest time in understanding how a vibrant queer cultural ecology would help your artists and audiences thrive.
* Create inclusive queer spaces. In the face of rising conservatism and lateral violence, the most radical thing we can do when creating queer spaces is to make them inclusive, safe and accessible.
* Cultivate a culture of using inclusive language. Ask yourself what will change the behaviour of those around you, spark their curiosity and make them care about the words they use.

✳ Be professional. Be careful not to conflate your social experience of being queer with your professional experience of being queer. Of course, there will always be crossover between personal and professional life, but how you behave in social situations is not how you should behave in work situations. Those you are working with deserve a professional environment to work in.

✳ Orient yourself. Set yourself a moral compass by listening to your communities. While it is impossible to please everyone, it is important to listen to the communities you are working with and to use these conversations to help orient you and your work.

Gender and public spaces

Simona Castricum and CQ Quinan

The public and private spaces we inhabit every day are gendered, but this often goes unnoticed. This invisible gendering upholds normative and binary frameworks of sex and gender, and strengthens cisnormative structures. It also affects how transgender, non-binary and gender-diverse communities experience public places – as well as the possibilities we have to design our own spaces.

By not thinking about the safety and comfort of gender-nonconforming people within our spaces, projects and institutions, we risk causing harm to communities and participants on the margins of access and power. Public spaces of risk include bathrooms, airports, prisons, and schools.

Terminology

These are terms that need to be understood in order to think about and discuss gender.

- Cisgender/Cis: People whose gender identity aligns with their sex assigned at birth
- Cisnormativity: The assumption that the male/female binary is 'normal' and 'natural' and that everyone is – or should be – cisgender, and that trans people are seen as inferior because they do not fit into mainstream gender norms

- Gender: The social and cultural meanings often ascribed to sex-based differences (for example, man, woman, masculinity, femininity)
- Gender diverse: Identities that diverge from normative or binary sex/gender identification, such as people who identify as transgender, gender-nonconforming, intersex or non-binary, as well as those who may have undergone a sex/gender transition or confirmation at some point in their lives but now identify along binary lines
- Non-binary: Individuals who do not identify within the gender/sex binary of man/woman or male/ female
- Sex: The range of physical, chromosomal, hormonal and anatomical differences that are usually used to describe the categories of male, female and intersex
- Trans: An umbrella term that includes all gender identities that transcend binary-gendered categories
- Transgender: People who identify with a gender other than that which was assigned to them at birth
- Transphobia: A behavioural prejudice that actively or inactively discriminates against or harms trans and gender-diverse people, communities or populations
- Administrative transphobia: How administrative processes lead to poor life outcomes that purposefully or unintentionally impact trans and gender diverse lives; systemic oppression that is inherently transphobic, hence the term 'administrative transphobia'.

Oppression through design

People of all genders are impacted by gendered design and architectural choices. However, trans and non-binary community members often experience public space differently from cisgender people. For gender-nonconforming people, simply navigating any urban public environment is routinely characterised by marginalisation and risk of discrimination and violence. This experience is rooted in harmful stereotypes about trans people and lives.

Place making – both as practice and as built environment – creates, defines and controls gendered spatial boundaries that segregate men and women and create little opportunity for those outside binary categories of gender. Building codes and other regulations can create challenges to inclusion and play a significant role in exacerbating discrimination. These biases and assumptions become replicated in the design of space.

The overt and invisible gendering of public spaces also creates an atmosphere in which transgender, non-binary and gender-diverse people are placed under constant surveillance. The cisnormative gaze renders the gender-nonconforming body suspicious or unworthy of admission. This often means that spaces themselves carry histories and archives of emotional affect that impact how trans people move through them. Effectively, this makes architecture and place making enabling of wider oppression.

For example, when gender-diverse people aren't involved in designing spaces that reflect autonomy and self-identity, or when building codes or legislation use discriminatory language to identify transgender, non-binary or gender-diverse people, they enact violence and administrative transphobia. Equally, organisations and institutions that uphold these dynamics and individuals who remain silent are complicit in discrimination and marginalisation. This has detrimental consequences for transgender, non-binary and gender-diverse people, and compromises our capacity to participate fully in civic life.

The opportunity for change lies in the relationship designers of spaces, projects and organisations have with the transgender, non-binary and gender-diverse community.

Co-designing safer spaces

The experiences of transgender, non-binary and gender-diverse people offer valuable lessons on how some spaces can be safe, supportive and welcoming, while others can be invasive, punitive and unsafe. Designers, programmers and practitioners working in community contexts must understand that transgender, non-binary and gender-diverse people have more to contribute to the built environment and public space than sharing stories about discrimination and violence or lobbying for better bathroom-user experiences.

It is critical to discuss the impact of place and space on all gender-nonconforming people in a way that looks beyond these issues and is more attentive to how our spaces, projects and organisations create both obstacles and possibilities for different genders.

What must we do to make spaces safer?

- Acknowledge and embrace that trans, non-binary and gender-diverse people exist everywhere.
- Think beyond diversity and inclusion to reconsider meaningful representation.
- Consider why trans, non-binary and gender-diverse people aren't reflected in our spaces' design.
- Ensure a diversity of experiences and perspectives in who is leading conversations about public and community space and place making.

Alternative and radical place-making methods are necessary to realise a future beyond the gender binary. To effect real change in trans lives, more significant agitation and advocacy are also required on issues of legislation, codes, policy and governance.

By listening to transgender, non-binary and gender-diverse people, our spaces, projects and organisations will be more inclusive of all types of bodies and identities that sit outside white, cisgender, heterosexual and non-disabled norms.

Public bathrooms

Denying trans people dignified access to bathrooms is stressful, exhausting and harmful. By demystifying the 'jargon' of architecture, designers can create accessible resources to assist gender-diverse people.

An example is the US-based project Stalled! by Joel Sanders, Susan Stryker and Terry Kogan, who in 2018 published findings of a three-year research project on bathroom accessibility for trans and gender-diverse people.

The project addresses the pressing social justice design issue of equitable and safer public restrooms.

Through an open-source online platform, their collaborative amenity- and retreat-focused bathroom design reframed conversations about public restroom access for transgender, non-binary and gender-diverse people. As an open online resource and a visual tool, Stalled! offers a significant precedent to foster discussions about public space and gender that centre the experiences of trans and gender-nonconforming users. This debate often sidelines the humanity and needs of trans people.

While Stalled! has yet to gain significant traction with designers and clients alike (groups that are largely made up of cisgender people), it is collaborative interdisciplinary projects like this that offer hope.

Sanders (an architect), Kogan (a lawyer) and Stryker (a trans historian and theorist) worked across disciplinary silos to address an urgent need of the trans, non-binary and gender-diverse community: safe bathroom access. Together, they formulated an inclusive design methodology, distilling user experience and design analysis to formulate best practice research. This led to understanding how critical shared design elements respond to the architectural and social challenge of universally accessible bathrooms. Materials, textures, signage, acoustics, walls, stalls, counters and fixtures respond to what Sanders describes as the cultural virtues of privacy, dignity, vision, abjection, shame and safety.

A design justice approach

US-based media scholar, participatory designer and activist Sasha Costanza-Chock offers a 'design justice' framework for analysing 'how design distributes benefits and burdens between various groups of people'.

A design-justice approach seeks to dismantle top-down systems and engage directly with the most marginalised communities, across differences in gender, race, ethnicity, ability, age and class. It also integrates social justice principles in which:

- transgender, non-binary and gender-diverse people can self-identify
- problems and challenges facing transgender, non-binary and gender-diverse communities in public spaces are taken seriously and addressed accordingly.

By recognising marginalised community members as uniquely skilled, their contributions are understood as opportunities for better design outcomes rather than obstacles.

Embracing a design-justice approach and trans design methodology can improve outcomes and life chances for trans, non-binary and gender-diverse people, increase visibility, and provide a space for inclusive storytelling. This can help break down myths, assumptions and stereotypes that undermine gender-nonconforming people and lead to futures of safety, belonging and permanence – part of a transformative social and cultural shift that takes concrete steps towards ending transphobia and discrimination against gender-nonconforming people.

....

Things to keep in mind

* In the current political climate where trans rights are being rescinded globally, transgender, non-binary and gender-diverse people need accomplices. Cisgender people must break down the systems of cisnormativity from which they benefit.
* Cisgendered assumptions are (often unconsciously) written into project briefs, spaces and events.
* Embrace participatory design and engagement with transgender, non-binary and gender-diverse people, and recognise their contributions, participation and expertise.
* Consult broadly with communities. Engage with and include transgender, non-binary and gender-diverse people at all stages of design and engagement.
* Give the microphone to transgender, non-binary and gender-diverse people while you become the audience and the listener.
* When designing spaces or planning events, consult best-practice guidelines that provide tools and strategies for working with and supporting trans, non-binary and gender-diverse communities. The following resources offer guidance on appropriate and inclusive language and encourage respectful attitudes toward trans artistry:

  ○ 'Clear expectations: Guidelines for institutions, galleries and curators working with trans, non-binary and gender diverse artists in Australia', by artists Spence Messih and Archie Barry.

○ 'Gender diversity draft strategy for best practice guidelines for live music venues', co-authored by Simona Castricum, Transgender Victoria and Queerspace.

✳ Create utopias and imagine conditions beyond our wildest dreams.

••

Regional arts practice:
Place takes time

Alysha Herrmann and
Anthony Peluso

What do we mean by 'regional arts practice'? Is it work
made in a regional location by city-based artists or
organisations? Or made in the city to tour to regional
areas? Or is it work made by regionally based artists
or about regional stories? What about if those regional
artists' work is only ever presented in the city?

Regional arts practice has long involved a series
of shifting definitions and provocative questions, which
encompasses all these scenarios (and more). At its heart
is the idea that whatever is being made or presented
could not happen in the way that it does anywhere else.
It is a creative moment that is embedded in and informed
by regional and remote locations, and the ways we are
shaped by place, irrespective of themes, art form or the
identity of the artists.

Whatever our definitions may be, making work
regionally requires deep thought before proceeding.
We want to avoid the mistakes and exploitation
of past practices and create regionally led work
that uplifts, celebrates, provokes, champions,
questions and empowers regional communities
to imagine, create and lead their own futures.

So, what might best practice look like? And how
can we strive together towards best practice, while

acknowledging that time, money, relationships and other factors mean we might not always achieve our own ideas of what that means? We should not shy away from wrestling with these questions and tensions. There is strength in difference and courage in not knowing all the answers. This is where best practice begins.

Best practice starts with 'why'

Why are you here? Why you? Why now? Why this? Why here?

When starting work on a regional arts project, we might not know all of the answers to these questions, and our answers might change over time. But asking them up front is an important part of the process. Our answers will shape how we make decisions, how we structure our practice and processes, who comes on the journey with us, and the kind of impact it will have. Interrogating our 'why' also leads to all sorts of other interesting questions:

- What benefit will you get from the project?
- How will it benefit others (regional artists, audiences and communities, the sector, etc.)?
- How will your regional arts practice support, question or challenge the existing power dynamics of the community you work in?
- Is the project something that can't be made anywhere else? How will making this work here and now – in this location, with this community, with these artists – be something that could only happen in this context?

Best practice requires us to check in with ourselves and deeply question our motivations and approach before we move forward. If we don't start with checking in, we risk forcing our own limited agendas onto place and community, and replicating models and ways of practice that erode trust, harm communities, and produce work that is flat, lifeless and trapped in stereotypes.

There is so much joy and so many benefits to regional arts practice: the relationships we forge along the way, the way our processes are shaped and shifted by the rhythms of the region, and the ways the outcomes are received locally and beyond. So, let's do it with care and respect.

Be part of the community

If we're working in our own community, knowing who to work with and how to work with them might seem obvious and easy, but there are just as many ways that we can be disconnected from our own places as there are ways we are connected to them. If we're working with a community we don't personally belong to, learning who is already working in this space and listening to how the community operates is a good way to begin.

Regional arts practice demands that we are engaged with local interests, ways of communicating, and the here and now of a place, including the critical lens of First Nations knowledge and experience, alongside the many complex histories each place holds. It's our responsibility to listen, learn and consider the ways our actions shape and are shaped by place.

Regional arts practice is also affected by the local landscape – the weather, the location, the distance from other places, and its quirks. All of this is essential for creating work that is unique, meaningful and grounded in the place where it's made. Sink into the place you are working and discover (or rediscover) being a local.

Ask, listen, share

Creative exchanges between artists and communities helps us build trust and make work that is relevant and exciting. This can be about sharing the ideology (why) of the work being explored or created, or sharing skills and opportunities for local engagement in the creative processes and outcomes.

Residencies can be a great way to offer moments where we can share our work and processes physically or online, and allow for dialogue with others in the place/s we work. Other ways of fostering exchange include workshops, talks, site visits or a cup of tea at the right place with the right people.

Create (and honour) time

Time can look different in different places, and with different people, and each regional community may have its own unique relationship with time. We have to be ready to listen to and understand time frames from a community's point of view, and be able and willing to build processes that align with these time frames. This might mean moving slower or faster than expected, or reordering what comes next.

Time should be considered in terms of process (how much time to allocate and over what period), as well as in the local natural cycles (such as First Nations ways of knowing and concepts of time, annual farming practices, vintage or other industry considerations, and local celebrations like footy finals, field days and local holidays).

Plan to have more time (or plan to do less) so that there is time for conversation, exchange and celebration. Some of the best processes include milestone moments for us to revisit the conversation and check in (with a play reading, drafts of work, sketches, etc.). We also want to celebrate the finished work in and with the place it was made. Time and how we use it are essential for building trust.

Work side by side

Sharing skills with each other in a two-way exchange (not from 'professional' to 'amateur') means that we all come away better off, with new insights and (hopefully) renewed inspiration to make more work.

Working side by side could look like paid collaborations between local and visiting artists, shadowing or placements for less experienced artists in the community, or practical skills sharing that builds legacy beyond the frame of the particular work we are making right now. This is essential for nurturing the sector, locally and more broadly, for the long term.

Keep measuring impact

To really understand our own practice (and improve it), we need to look critically at our own ways of working and what we've produced, and how this informs the next steps for everyone involved. What has worked, what hasn't and why?

Measuring impact means thinking about how much you did, how well you did it, and if/how anyone is better off. Without this, success might just be wishful thinking. This includes capturing the initial set of outcomes: what was made, how it was received, what skills were learnt/ exchanged, and how this might influence future work and opportunities.

The challenge we all continue to wrestle with is capturing impact in an ongoing way. This is where the value of long-term relationships is most keenly felt. Do communities trust us? Do they want to work with us again? Are they having ideas and driving new work for themselves? What does a place look and feel like five years after our project ends? What about after ten years? Or 20?

The answers to these questions are all clues to our success, and part of the ongoing and circular process of regional arts practice. Measuring impact takes us back to where we started: how well we did on our 'why'.

Things to keep in mind

* Ask lots of questions at the beginning. If this is not your regional community, why are you working here? Should you be working here?
* As with all practice, consider intersectionality in the ways that you work. How can you use your privilege and power to build process and practice that dismantles structural inequality?
* Consider power dynamics when bringing in outside expertise. Who has decision-making power and how has that been negotiated?
* Barriers for community engagement/participation are amplified in most regional contexts. Budget accordingly.
* Make and take time. Move at the pace of community.
* Foster two-way exchange in what you do and in how you do it.
* Design for the context you are working in, not the context you wish you were working in.
* Make space and time to celebrate.
* Think strategically about partners, money and time. How does your work contribute to shared impact?
* Follow up with audiences, partners and artists after the project/consultation/event is over. Ask them what impact it had. Ask them how you can do better. Ask them what they want to do next. Offer your own reflections generously and with care.
* Celebrate what we can do in the regions that we cannot do anywhere else. It's OK for it not to make sense to people in the city or in other communities.

No-one here talks about class

Nina Ross, Lizzy Sampson
and Jessie Scott

We don't talk about class much in Australia, which means
it can be tricky to get our heads around it. Terms like
'working class' and 'middle class' are familiar, but what
do they actually mean? And how do they play out when
working with communities or participating in the arts?

Class is a way of dividing people in society. It is
loosely measured and determined by three types of
'capital': what you do (cultural capital), who you know
(social capital) and what you have (economic capital).
The existence of this class structure enables inequality,
disadvantage and classism, but it is often invisible or
overlooked (particularly for those who benefit from it).
Colonisation continues to embed inequalities where race
and class intersect to compound disadvantage, as does
ableism and the barriers to access faced by those who
also experience class disadvantage.

In the arts, these three buckets of 'class capital'
overlap and interweave enormously. For artists, economic
capital directs what you can produce, which materials
you can use, and how much time you can dedicate to
your artistic work. For arts workers, the amount of capital
you have may determine your ability to take up unpaid
internships, low waged professional positions or unpaid

training opportunities, which greatly impact career progression.

An individual's class privilege can easily feed into the organisations they work for. Organisations can then face challenges, such as a lack of diversity or boards that don't reflect the communities they represent. As a result, communities may then be restricted to participating in opportunities that don't feel socially or culturally relevant, don't reflect their values, or which are inaccessible. Social, economic and cultural capital play a huge and vital role in the success of individual careers and projects. Who you know, what you can produce, and where you and your work are seen are all capital essential to success.

How does class play out in the arts?

There are often huge economic disparities between who is making art and who is commissioning, experiencing or viewing art, but class introduces another complex layer that can be a barrier for some and not others.

While research shows that 98 per cent of Australians engage with the arts in some way, both attendance and creative participation in the arts decreases with household income. In a 2015 poll from the Australian National University (ANU), one of the measures of a higher class status was participation in the arts – whether that be attending the opera or listening to hip hop. In this study, the arts were defined as 'highbrow', and participation was used as a measure of class.

These results could point to an 'image problem' within the arts, which many arts workers and community practitioners are keen to shake off. In reality, the vast definition of 'arts participation' concurrently reflects a vastness of experiences, such as whether the experience has contributed to a sense of connectedness to community or whether participation has been passive or active.

Class is more than 'rich versus poor'

The complexities of class privilege and disadvantage are measured by more than our socio-economic status. Factors such as our ability to access tertiary education, the distance we live from metropolitan areas, access to transport, or our lived experience of trauma, displacement or migration all contribute to class privilege or disadvantage.

Our status can also change over time depending on a multitude of circumstances. For example, you could inherit money or a debt, become a single parent overnight, lose access to your community as a result of migration, or lose your ability to work.

Some of us experience class every day, being acutely aware of our perceived place on the rungs of society's ladder. Others are blissfully unaware – a tell-tale sign that they're probably in a pretty comfortable position. Class is least visible to people who don't need to worry about it – those who have intergenerational wealth, double incomes, housing stability or few caring responsibilities.

The regular request of artists to work for 'exposure' rather than being paid properly and fairly for their labour enables those with class privilege to take up opportunities that people with class disadvantage may need to turn down. Artists are rarely paid enough to make a living wage, yet the reputation that the arts in Australia are elite or highbrow remains.

Theatres, galleries and other arts institutions that charge a fee for entry are more obviously exclusive to those with disposable income (think blockbuster international shows), but most of our public and commercial galleries, while free to enter, still have a whiff of elitism about them: language inaccessibility can imply that visitors behave in a certain way, meaning some people feel like they don't belong in those spaces.

As community practitioners, accessible, meaningful arts experiences require deep reflection about what mechanisms need to be in place to ensure equitable participation, which goes beyond free entry.

Hidden privilege

Despite the fact that aspects of the arts are free, available and 'accessible', the reputation of the arts as a classist enclave continues. The concentration of privilege in the arts means our own classism remains largely invisible to ourselves.

At first, it can be difficult to spot classism in the arts, probably because it begins early. In a sector that on its face is committed to social justice, equality and equal representation, what are some of the mechanisms by which class rigs the game?

The communities we are born into can have a big impact on both exposure and access to the arts. Following this, there is a clear contrast between the resources that private and public school students have access to and what sort of works they can produce in the early stages of pursuing a career. This advantage flows into tertiary study, where huge fee debts are racked up for non-vocational degrees – often inaccessible to students from low-income or otherwise disadvantaged families.

Those with a cushion of intergenerational wealth may be able to withstand increasing costs of living with free or subsidised rent in family properties, requiring them to work less hours at a day job or enabling them to commit more time and disposable income to their studies, art work or careers.

Social connections, tertiary-educated families who offer financial support, better-paid professional spouses, inheritances and trust funds often underpin successful artists who seemingly come fully formed out of nowhere. In a highly competitive, under-resourced industry, these passive, less visible resources are a huge advantage for practising artists and arts workers. This situation is exacerbated by gender, cultural diversity and disability, with corresponding issues around low pay and low status, and risks making arts sectors bubbles of class privilege.

Does this mean everyone who succeeds does so because of unearned, unacknowledged privilege? No, of course not. But if we are unaware of class privilege and class disadvantage (and how these intersect with a range of other factors), we may fall prey to making assumptions about other people's access to resources, further entrenching inequality.

Let's talk about money (and power)

But how do we address something that goes largely unacknowledged or unseen?

There is a hesitance in this industry to raise our voices and ask for things to be fairer, more equitable, or just more available – and so an unequal system continues to entrench itself unchallenged. Part of this is a reluctance to talk about money. We might talk about it in the abstract, on panels, podcasts or articles like this. But people who work in for-purpose industries like the arts will often turn themselves inside out to avoid letting money become an obstacle to their success.

As people working with communities, we often find ourselves managing inadequate or 'shoestring' budgets. These shortfalls have a knock-on effect, rendering the ability to support meaningful community participation very difficult. An inadequate budget can impact community participation in a myriad ways: it may mean that communications don't extend beyond online platforms or an inability to provide transport for isolated communities.

A powerful notion that holds sway in the arts is that there is not enough money to pay artists properly, the culture creators who bring people into cities and towns all around Australia to spend money in the broader economy. But if you work within a cultural institution as an arts administrator, curator, programmer or community facilitator, chances are you are being paid. So, it is important that you are aware of the power dynamic when you are representing an organisation that is working with artists and communities – relying on them, even, to ensure your project's success. Are you asking communities to invest in unpaid labour? Is there a cost involved for communities to access your venue or project, and is this a barrier? Are there additional resources you can offer the community, such as access to equipment, organisational knowledge, materials or physical space to connect with other participants?

Not talking openly about money propels people to accept punishing conditions that are unsustainable, in order to avoid upsetting or being passed over by the polite upper-middle-class milieu of the institutions they are working with or for. This enables exploitation to continue, and can create a barrier that determines a community's ability to participate.

We have to normalise asking for fair treatment:

- 'That's not enough money to do what you're asking me to do.'
- 'We need to provide a budget for childcare (or to cover other caring responsibilities) so all of our artists and participants can take part.'
- 'How can I prioritise resources to enable opportunities for community participants who are hard to reach or under-represented?'

Artists and community-engaged practitioners need to have these conversations proactively, receive them graciously and be prepared to respond.

....

Things to keep in mind

* Check your privilege, continuously, on every project or community interaction.
* Have you proactively consulted with the communities you are working with to ensure equitable opportunities for different demographics? Ensure you offer accommodations rather than relying on communities to ask for them.
* Does intergenerational privilege enable your art practice? Understand and remember that your class privilege doesn't extend to many other people you are working with. If you don't have the required understanding or knowledge about working with communities experiencing class disadvantage, ensure you have someone on your project team who does.
* Normalise talking about your project fees with your peers and the institution or community you are working with. Be an advocate for enabling community participation and access by agitating for fair pay and adequate budgets that include things like childcare, community transport and far-reaching communications.
* Do you have a stable job working for or with a particular community? Prioritise offering the resources you have as a salaried staffer to the community and artists you are working with, such as offering space, time, materials, technology, printing services or institutional knowledge.

....

The role of the institution

Esther Anatolitis

Arts organisations exist to support artists to focus
on their practice. They secure resources, facilitate
relationships, manage risks, promote work and develop
audiences.

As organisations have grown and become more
sophisticated, and the arts sector has become a complex
industry, institutions have emerged in all art forms:
from galleries, festivals and performing arts companies,
to sector service organisations, education and funding
bodies. These arts institutions are more than just
organisations. They work with more than one group of
artists, across a region, state or country, with a focus
on an entire sector of the arts. Their strategic vision,
programming decisions and communications are aimed
at a broad, diverse public. Their work goes beyond direct
support and towards cultural leadership – whether that
kind of leadership is recognised by the institution or not.
They put the public good ahead of making money. And
they promote values that influence our culture. In other
words, they have power.

But how seriously does the institution take its
power? How can it recognise and apply that power to
its daily focus as well as its future direction? And does it
understand which communities of artists and audiences
it is ultimately responsible to?

The role of the artist

The history of the power of the arts institution is the history of co-opting the power of the artist.

Artists define what's possible and defy what's impossible. Artists ask questions that unsettle what we see and how we think. They make work with rigour and care, drawing on cultural traditions that are as old as time, and exploding them in unknowable directions.

Artists choose where and how to make and show their work. They're not limited by the way that public, commercial or private spaces are commonly understood. They use their curiosity to take risks, and those risks inspire our own curiosity. Artists inspire us to choose what we value for ourselves, to rethink our role in creating our own culture.

The work of artists brings people together – perhaps accidentally, as people experience an artwork together, or perhaps on purpose, in collaborating with a community of people to make something new. Community-engaged artists guide us in daring to express our hopes, fears and passions, and to discover others who share these values – others who are just as willing to act on them. This means that when an institution develops or presents the work of artists, it takes an active role in creating social values. It takes the creative power of the artist and transforms it into something else.

Cultural power

Let's look at the cultural power of the institution more closely.

Today's arts institutions can choose whose stories to tell, whose work to collect, which work to develop and which to promote. In offering jobs, they can decide (or not) to strengthen gender equity and cultural diversity, provide meaningful work in a stimulating workplace, and pay fairly. In presenting awards or granting funds, they can say what makes for excellent work, or what work should be made. Or they can speak on someone else's behalf, offer expertise and influence government policy.

In making these choices, institutions have the power to define communities, frame art-form boundaries, determine accessibility, develop careers and confer status. These choices set national standards and champion public values. In other words, they are political.

Arts institutions don't tend to think of themselves as having political responsibility. They see themselves as politically inert. But if we look at their fundamental purpose, we are reminded that the institution is founded on the basis of its public benefit. Its constitution directs that work to the communities it serves. It must serve more than just a paid membership if it receives public funding. It must serve communities beyond those it has defined, constantly seeking to diversify audiences. And it must ensure it has written policies around accessibility and gendered harassment, for example. More than just part of managing an organisation, these are the key elements of cultural power: the power to shape public values.

Power and responsibility

This cultural power of institutions cannot be shirked, but it can be exposed as fraudulent when they don't uphold gender equity, accessibility or cultural diversity; when they don't pay artists fairly; or when they don't pay artists at all.

Even when that power is fraudulent – even when it has been shown to have no basis in ethics or science or truth – it continues to operate effectively, as Australia's culture wars show us every day. And yet the power of the institution to build careers, endow prestige and add value to the work of art is very real.

These are critical times. Every one of us has the power to call this out and change it for the better. We can do that by asking to see those written policies – around accessibility, gendered harassment, artist payment, strategic partnerships or public advocacy. As participants in membership-based organisations, we can learn more about how board members make decisions from what the minutes of board meetings record, or we might even run for a board position ourselves.

In the same way that we seek to understand political decision-makers as citizens and then use our vote wisely, we can make sure that institutional power is something that's openly discussed among our communities. We can keep those conversations going, tracing a clear line from the work of the artist to the work of the institution, and understanding that line as a continuity or a discontinuity of ethics and values.

Community-engaged practice displaces the power of the institution by strengthening the agency of communities. The future of the arts institution is the story of the power of the artist.

··

Things to keep in mind

An institution that thinks through the following questions will be one that is ready to articulate and defend its ethics under any circumstances. One that understands when to stand up – and when to stand aside. One that recognises that its power is entirely dependent on those who come together with courage and ethical conviction to create new work.

* What are the institution's values? What comes through in their job ads, programming decisions and social media? Are those values gendered? Do they privilege non-disabled people? Do they welcome cultural diversity? What values do they say they uphold, and what values do they really uphold? Are they putting First Nations first, last or nowhere at all?

* Does the institution claim to speak on someone else's behalf? What practices do they normalise? What cultures do they privilege? What are they resigned to, what have they settled over, what do they control and what do they seek to change?

* Does the institution employ people fairly? Do they pay artists? Do they have a written policy on artist payment? Do they pay according to industry standards?

* Does the institution understand risk as core to its purpose – not reducing or eliminating risk, but doing everything in its power to support the work of artists? Does it instead leverage its power to pass business risks on to artists? What kind of work does this create? What kind of work does this deny? Are artists having to indemnify or pay to insure against the institution's practices? What position does this

put the artist in when it comes to working with community members volunteering their time, or collaborating in spaces that are culturally significant and safe for communities?

* How does the institution make decisions? Who is on its board and how were they appointed? Who is employed there, how did they get their jobs, and how long do they tend to stay? What does the institution do to foster reflection and criticism as part of a healthy workplace culture?

* How ready is the institution to lead? What's their position when it comes to championing public values? Do they think a politically neutral position is possible? Do they understand that claiming political neutrality is itself a colonising statement, a protection of privilege?

* How ready is the institution to respond? When it's necessary to defend public values, will it take a stand? What's its position on artists' rights? Is it silent or vocal during politicised attacks? Is it active or inactive on anti-racism and gender equity? Is it visible or invisible to the public agenda?

* When the institution talks about 'community', is it only ever in opposition to 'excellence', as though the two are mutually exclusive? Who are its communities? To whom is the institution responsible? And how can we know?

· ·

The role of festivals

Anna Reece

Festivals are a celebration of ideas, culture and vitality.
They can surprise, provoke and inspire us. They
are gathering grounds, bringing people together to
collectively share an experience. They remind us to keep
an open mind and heart, feeding our curiosity about
the world and encouraging us to allow that curiosity
to override our fears.

Festivals produce and exchange knowledge, stories
and cultural perspectives. They create a sense of
belonging. They disrupt and transform. They can show
us the world and make us think about how we live in it.

Festivals magnify communities for a fleeting moment
in time. They can be spaces for meaning, encounters and
collaboration, as well as spaces for hope and for change.
They should allow artists to dream, take risks, and
encourage audiences to embrace them.

The joy of a festival is the permission we give
ourselves to share art and tell stories in unconventional
spaces. They can create a unique environment that invites
communities to meet and talk with each other on a
common ground – be it a picnic blanket, a plush red seat
or a pile of sand.

It is who they gather, how they gather, what they
share, and how it is experienced that determines the
kinds of festivals they will be. As curators, programmers
and festival makers, we are given the privileged position

of deciding what has value and a place in that space. However, we must never forget that we have a community holding us accountable.

The festival life cycle

The power of a festival sits directly with the community in which it is placed.

Whether they are community-based, international, curated, fringe, multi-disciplinary or art-form focused, the origins of festivals range from cultural and religious celebrations to feasts, rituals and ceremonies, natural disasters and tragedies. All stem from a desire to share. All are moments in time where one community can be in dialogue with many others and potentially create something extraordinary.

Festival models are flexible. You can bend them without breaking them. As a community shifts and changes, so, too, should their festivals. A one-size-fits-all model does not exist and cannot be applied. A healthy festival will interrogate and scrutinise. Our duty of care is to be specific. Each festival must carefully develop its own unique formula to ensure it responds to and reflects its own community, society and place.

Festivals used to be one of the few moments that would bring the world to our door and encourage us to experience and explore it. Today's endless digital entertainment options provide us with little need to leave our homes. The festivals that will survive this technology will be those that are deeply embedded in their communities and that successfully demonstrate the impact of a shared experience.

The role of festival makers

Festival makers are the people in between.
We are connectors, bridge builders and mediators.
As festival makers, we must use the privilege we
have to make space for those who don't. The choices
we make will inevitably mean we are excluding
someone. Ask yourself these questions over and
over again and the festival will ground itself:

- Who are we impacting?
- Who are we excluding?
- How can we make space?

Programming with our hearts open to these
questions is sensitive and risk taking, innovative
and brave. It is the future of festival making.

A festival should be a caretaker of stories, not a
sole storyteller. Don't try to tell someone else's story.
Let those storytellers speak. This is the true magic a
festival can create: a space to share stories.

The festivals that will thrive will be those that
program with their communities (not for them) and that
explore new models of artistic leadership and operation.
Those that do so will remain connected, relevant and
unique, continuing to hold space and support. Those that
don't will see their relevance diminish; their community
will lose interest.

Regardless of how they started or how long they've been around, all festivals have life cycles. They can age, they can deplete, they can die or they can regenerate. It is the community who holds the power to decide. It is time for festivals to stop prioritising those demographics who reflect our past and not our future.

The impact of festivals

By their very nature, festivals create impact. They offer a localised conversation in a global context and a global conversation in a local context. They are a powerful tool for cultural dissemination and mutual understanding.

A festival's mission is local. But in a highly politicised and increasingly polarised world, there is a growing need to humanise and naturalise different narratives that are not being heard.

Festivals are not audience engagement strategies. They are a critical act of community building and can be an extraordinarily emotional platform. We need to consider what kind of spaces we are creating for our community:

- Who is the work for?
- What connections can the festival make with those communities before the work is presented?
- How do we curate space for difficulty?
- How do we curate a space where discomfort is OK but doesn't escalate?
- What steps should we take to ensure there is support or a pathway for anyone who feels triggered?

Curation of a festival is about navigating space and place making. A successful festival strikes a balance between what it means to celebrate place and people – creating experiences where our communities feel the joy of belonging while addressing the urgency of today. We must navigate the critical balance of keeping our memories alive while also looking forward.

Festivals can gift us a plurality of voices. Through access to a diverse offering of arts and culture, a festival can help us create empathy, generate mutual respect, or support the ability to listen at a larger level. They can encourage us not to shut out dissent or differing points of view.

If we don't lean into difficult and uncomfortable conversations, our world won't grow or evolve. Festivals can (and should) play a critical role in creating space for those conversations to take place.

A festival can also be a joyful intervention between artists and audiences. Artists can redefine who or what they can be, take risks, and encourage audiences to embrace new things. Festivals can allow artists to showcase their work to audiences that they would traditionally not have been able to access and to use that experience to develop their practice.

....

Things to keep in mind

Creating your festival with the following questions in mind will position you well to reflect the diversity and vitality of your community:

* Country. Consider the Country upon which the festival will be staged and the culture embedded within it. How

can the festival celebrate, recognise and integrate
First Nations culture?

* Structure. Festivals began because a community
  had a reason or desire to congregate. Yet many have
  evolved into large, highly hierarchical structures.
  A festival is an alliance of ideas and its structure
  should reflect that. When considering the ideal
  organisational or curatorial structure for a festival,
  our boards, people and programs must reflect the
  diversity of the community we are placed within.

* Place. Festivals use art to transform people's
  relationship to place. They can explore, open up
  and share spaces in ways we have not considered
  or experienced before. Creating or presenting art
  in these spaces can give people and communities a
  shared experience and connection to place. Consider
  also how you can leave a legacy of newly discovered
  spaces for artists to continue to use.

* Impact. A festival doesn't have to be an ephemeral
  thing that appears and disappears. Yet, critically, it
  is not an institution or a venue. A healthy festival
  will have lasting impact and a strong connection
  to its community year-round, regardless of its
  core activity. Consider the reciprocal 'pipe line' of
  your festival into the community – partnerships,
  artistic collaborations, engagement with education
  or training institutions – and nurture those
  relationships before and after the festival takes
  place.

* Objectivity. Keeping an open mind is a hard thing to
  do, but festivals must. Our communities will always
  have different perspectives and perceptions. People
  come to a festival for a shared experience. It is our

role to share work that gives people an opportunity to participate.

* Consent. Festivals should have consent and authenticity front of mind. Who is a festival responsible to? What consultation has taken place with community? How will this inform the making of the festival? Does your curatorial approach reflect an intimate understanding of your community context? How will the community remain engaged in the decision-making process?

* Access. When considering what work to present in a festival, ask yourself and others: why do you want to share it? Who is it for? Who will go and why? Who won't go and why (and how will we get them there)? Are we being inclusive? Are we accessible?

* Scale. Bigger does not necessarily mean better. If conversations shift to scale and size, question the motivation before you act.

* Context. Consider your local context, your local artistic community, and your city. Ask yourself:

  O What is the heartbeat of the festival? Who is it for? Why does it exist?
  O Who are the protagonists of the festival (such as emerging artists, young people, etc.)?
  O What are the partnerships you can form to ensure the festival is embedded in a community?

* Culture. Are we doing enough to reflect what our society and culture are all about?

* Ethos. A festival does not build communities. It is communities that build a festival.

Platforming for community: Going beyond surface representation

Adolfo Aranjuez

Whether we're talking about race, gender, sexuality, disability or class, many communities are called 'minorities' because they have a perceived 'minor' influence on society. But we're at a point in history where minorities are pushing against the disempowerment they have long suffered. Calls for more and better representation can't be ignored.

This upheaval is strongly felt within the arts, a sector that has both aesthetic and ethical dimensions. Works of art show us how we are and how we could be. As the saying goes, 'If you can't see it, you can't be it'. Without *Star Trek* character Uhura, for example, Mae Jemison would never have become the first African-American astronaut in space.

Visibility is power: the more you're seen, the more you're seen to be important. But being seen can be difficult, and being seen in the way that we want, even more so. Diversity box ticking and quotas provide a simplistic answer to a complex problem. How do we make sure that representation in panels, performances, forums or exhibitions is truly empowering?

Empowerment can come from engaging and collaborating with minorities. Equity can be achieved by elevating minority voices and needs.

Nothing about us without us

When fighting for a specific group, we must prioritise the voices of its members. In discussions of social justice, this is known as 'centring'. These people have lived through the hardships we're opposing, after all, so they have the most authority on those issues.

The mantra 'nothing about us without us' became well known through the work of disability-rights activist James I. Charlton in the 1990s. The statement itself is rich in meaning. 'About us' reminds us of how often minorities are 'spoken for' by governments and others who believe they know what's 'best'. In effect, though, this silences minorities' voices and can distort our understanding of their needs. 'Without us' is a cry for inclusion – not through token representation but direct participation. 'Nothing' clarifies that minorities should always govern their own lives, without exception.

Empowerment: Reframing representation

Diversity box ticking and quotas can easily lead to a scramble for individuals expected to speak 'on behalf of' their entire community. Even if by accident, this paints a complex group with the same simplistic brush. In the end, this is a hollow gesture that only gives the appearance of representation.

No minority group is made up of carbon copies of the same person. Experiences of inequality can also differ if a person lives with intersecting types of disadvantage. Diversity exists not just between communities (for instance, LGBTQIA+ people versus straight people) but also within them (cisgender gay men versus non-binary trans queers). The people in these groups have individual values, dreams and perspectives, and their obstacles to success can vary. By relying on just a single 'representative', newer voices or different perspectives can be drowned out.

In the best-case scenario, minorities will self-represent through projects run by their own communities or headed by them within mainstream organisations. This isn't about forming 'ghettos' within the arts, with group members only making work with and for that group. Rather, this is about achieving representation that is truly empowering. 'Outsiders' to the group can still enjoy the work, but that work will be more authentic as it is community-led.

Engagement: The numbers game

We often rely on percentages to assess how 'representative' we're being. Mainly, we do this by comparing the composition of hired creatives against population figures.

Percentages offer a helpful lens for kickstarting discussion. But we can't rely on the numbers game, which reduces people to statistics using a single metric. A person from anywhere in Asia counts as 'Asian', ignoring cultural differences across the continent or other identity markers like gender and class.

On one hand, statistics can give us quick and easy snapshots of areas we can improve. On the other hand, they can trick us into thinking we've reached solutions when numbers go up. For example, arts organisations habitually celebrate having equal numbers of men and women in their latest ventures. A worthwhile accomplishment indeed. But were they counting individual women or merely the presence of a female staff member on a project (which could well be the same woman each time)? Did these women have authority among their collaborators to call the shots? How many of them were first-time or emerging artists? Which of them were minorities in other ways (non-white, non-heterosexual, non-cisgender or disabled)?

A percentage increase, like a box in a checklist, gives the sense of an endpoint. In terms of representation, we end up asking, 'Have we included X group?' and just aiming for the answer 'Yes'. But numbers only show a small part of the big picture. As they neglect intersectional factors, they don't tell us about in-group diversity or longer-term change.

Elevation: Platforms with purpose

More and more people are beginning to understand both the political and economic power of representation. Over the past decade, Hollywood films with diverse characters and storylines have done increasingly well at the box office. We've seen an uptick in 'diverse'-led shows, discussions and organisations. But often, these projects are led by minority veterans who've mastered how to 'perform' for the mainstream. These veterans' position of relative power comes down to 'cultural capital'. Much like financial capital, cultural capital is accumulated throughout someone's career. And like with money, the people with more cultural capital end up having more power.

In this way, the arts industry is similar to a bank. It's less 'risky' to invest with a wealthier client, and it's similarly less 'risky' to offer a diversity platform to 'the usual suspects'. What's more, the industry now sees diversity as a worthy investment and can exploit it to sell tickets. This is known as 'identity capitalism'. If wielded harmfully, it can actually worsen inequality.

Receiving a platform, commission, contract or tenure offers visibility and prestige, resulting in more cultural capital. But minorities have access to only a small number of platforms. This is why it's vital that minority individuals in positions of influence engage in what I call 'platforming'.

A less capitalistic approach to opportunities, platforming can be achieved in a number of ways. It could involve using your own cultural capital to create new platforms for others so they can gain cultural capital themselves. Or it could involve turning down a platform and recommending another community member who needs uplifting.

Of course, minorities shouldn't have to refuse work when the fault lies with an unjust system. The goal is to surpass platforms that tick boxes (and sustain the status quo). Until we get there, though, platforming can be a leaping-off point towards larger collective change. Through it, more minority individuals can build the necessary cultural capital to do well in the arts sector and beyond.

Things to keep in mind

There's no one-size-fits-all way to achieve equal representation. But here are some steps in the right direction:

* Clarity of intention. Are you simply trying to raise awareness? Do you want to amplify prominent voices or shine a spotlight on lesser-known ones? Do you want to influence outsiders or refine in-group perspectives?
* Purposeful consultation. How have you accounted for the group's needs and interests? Did you rely on existing (sometimes stereotyped) media/societal narratives, or did you check with members of the group directly? Have you asked group elders and leaders for suggestions? Were you really listening during consultations, rather than imposing your own or your audience's assumptions?
* Reciprocal collaboration. What do the communities you work with get in return? Does it benefit them tangibly, or are you just looking to meet your own needs? Do they have equal footing to push back on any terms you've set?
* Purposeful content. Many panels still discuss (the fact of) diversity despite minority communities criticising them. We've also seen shows that are 'colourblind' or 'gender-swapped' but these just sidestep rather than address a lack of representation. What is your goal in 'talking about diversity' or papering over a historical problem? Could you instead present diverse viewpoints on different topics or pathways for newer stories?
* Bigger picture. Are you addressing societal factors like access, language or culture? What does this project offer that existing ones don't, or how can you tie into those other initiatives? (Be careful of taking time and resources away from existing projects that you could support or partner with. Remember that minority platforms are hard to come by!)

* Targeted delivery. Who are you trying to reach?
  How will you reach that audience?
* Follow-through. Have you set up processes and
  relationships so your minority collaborators feel
  supported? How will you avoid them feeling they've
  been exploited or thrown into the deep end?
* Invested evaluation. Have you set up protocols
  to evaluate your success (beyond the 'numbers
  game')? How will you measure the impact of your
  work? Once you've finished, how can you make the
  collaboration sustainable and not just a one-off act
  of 'representation'?

....

Audiences and cultural diversity

Fotis Kapetopoulos

Cultural diversity in the arts is often focused on what is presented on stage and screens, but far less consideration is given to the cultural diversity of audiences. In fact, the issue of engagement with diverse cultural communications and communities continues to be avoided by many. Are arts administrators ignoring culturally diverse audiences, or are these audiences ignoring the arts?

Setting the scene

The language used to describe non-Indigenous Australians that don't come from Anglo-British backgrounds has changed over time, reflecting the reality of post–World War II migration and the development of official multicultural policies.

'Ethnic' began to be used in the 1970s and 1980s, followed by 'non-English-speaking backgrounds (NESB)' in the 1990s. Currently, terms like 'culturally and linguistically diverse (CALD)', 'culturally diverse', 'multicultural' and 'ethnic' are all regularly used. More recently, 'People of Colour (POC)' has entered as an import from America. Regardless of the terms we use to describe ourselves, the depth and growth of Australia's multicultural communities cannot and should not be ignored.

Immigration is the main contributor to Australia's growing population, with overseas migration bringing more than 200 000 people into the country each year. According to 2021 census data from the Australian Bureau of Statistics, 28 per cent of Australians were born overseas, and 48 per cent have one or both parents who were born overseas. Population research group .id noted that the top languages other than English spoken at home in 2021 were Mandarin, Arabic, Vietnamese, Cantonese, Punjabi, Greek, Italian, Filipino/Tagalon, Hindi and Spanish.

Multicultural Australians know that art and culture define their core identity. Our multicultural communities have well-established infrastructures with community centers, financial services, doctors, lawyers, media, schools, dance, music and theatre ensembles, and arts and cultural festivals.

Ethnic festivals are platforms for established and emerging artists and are used by our governments to promote our diverse cities and regions. They draw large audiences and add to local economies. And there is no shortage of politicians keen to open them.

The real challenge

In choosing not to market to, or engage with, multicultural communities, a significant and growing market is left untapped.

The government-funded arts industry is one of the few sectors in Australia not to have actively taken on multicultural marketing. Communicating with culturally diverse audiences is too often considered as an optional outreach activity, or a response to a focus on access and equity. However, this approach largely ignores the economic, intellectual, and political power of multicultural communities.

Australia's many multicultural festivals receive little arts funding and are, overall, ignored by arts organisations as opportunities for research, collaboration, and audience development. It is not often that we see ethnic festivals secure funding from arts funders, or arts organisations enlisting the support of ethnic festivals.

When campaigns targeting specific communities can be found, they often present those communities as homogenous. And yes, language, history, traditions, faith, and what UNESCO describes as 'intangible cultural heritage' do result in some homogeneity. But not everyone within these communities is the same. Geography (both in their original homelands or in Australia), their period of settlement, class, age, gender, disability, sexuality, faith, class and education levels all make the definition of audience segments complex.

Some audience diversification campaigns tend to engage with hyper-visible groups like refugees, or groups deemed as needing more assistance. This means that larger and/or more established communities, as well as less-visible immigrants from other areas, can be ignored. Yet these groups may have the financial capacity and time to be involved as audiences and have access to political and economic power that may be useful in a partnership with arts organisations.

Ethnic media (in English and other languages) is vital to the cultural and political sustenance of culturally diverse communities. Ethnic media outlets – including newspapers, radio and online – are deep and diverse. They are an excellent source of promotions and publicity, and natural advocates for arts projects. They are often made up of family-owned businesses that maintain deep historical links to the community they service and have significant inter-generational networks. In Victoria alone, ethnic media communicates to over 1.5 million people each month. But despite being a vital engagement partner, ethnic media is rarely used by the arts.

Economics and class are often cited as barriers to attendance. Australian political author George Megalogenis writes that we are currently experiencing the largest wave of skilled, middle-class migration since the mid-19th century – from India, England, China, South Africa and the Philippines.

After World War II, immigrant waves of Italians and Greeks, then Vietnamese and Lebanese, all started on the 'lower rungs of the income ladder and we measured their integration through their uptake of small business and home ownership and the success of their Australian-born children through education'. However, 21st-century immigration 'inverted the relationship between new arrival and host, as our ethnic face changes from Anglo-European to Eurasian'. Megalogenis writes that the new arrivals are younger and better educated, and land between the middle and the top of the income ladder:

Two out of every three new arrivals since 2001 have been skilled immigrants. They come primarily from India, England, China, South Africa and the Philippines, to work as doctors and nurses, human-resources and marketing professionals, business managers, IT specialists, and engineers.

The arts must recognise the aspirational nature of these immigrants, and that they experience greater upward mobility than the children born of long-term Anglo heritage.

Engaging with culturally diverse audiences is also an ethical imperative, given the taxes of culturally diverse Australians go towards funding our cultural ecology.

An invitation to the party

America's leader in audience diversification Donna Walker-Kuhne created an approach of 'inviting people to the table' that she used to bridge the historic divide between African American audiences and Broadway musicals. The idea was developed when working for the Public Theater in New York, when the director of the leading theatre company asked Walker-Kuhne to make their foyer as diverse as a New York subway station.

To achieve that invitation, Walker-Kuhne notes that multicultural audience development needs to be embedded within an organisation's mission and supported from the boardroom to front of house. Engagement and promotional activities need to be taken into communities (rather than waiting for them to come to us).

Walker-Kuhne reminded us that 'multicultural audiences don't need you, they are doing fine'. But they do need to feel 'invited' into an arts house or activity. She says, 'We took [the show] wherever there was a gathering of people, so that the product, the cast, the show, and the concept was accessible to people in their own neighbourhood'.

Pop-up performances, workshops, meet-and-greet events, and activities in schools, churches, businesses and community associations can also help create awareness and make people feel like they are invited to the party. Hospitality is a serious aspect of political and social engagement.

Things to keep in mind

* There needs to be a shift from only using access and equity as the drivers of diverse community engagement. Multicultural communities do not need assistance; the arts need communities as allies, audiences and collaborators.
* Arts organisations need to include engagement and communications with diverse audiences, patrons and communities in their vision (and support it from the top down).
* Research is essential. A greater awareness of culture, language, region, class and faith as motivations to consumption makes a difference in the way one communicates to different segments of each community.
* Understand the interests and aspirations of the communities you want to target. Multicultural Australians do not have their cultural and

entertainment consumption determined by their cultural and linguistic background. However, an awareness of culture, language and faith as motivations to consumption makes a difference in the way we communicate to multicultural market segments.

* Employ people with expertise in multicultural marketing, ethnic media relations and engagement.
* Build relationships with professional associations, women's and cultural associations, and language schools.
* Invite community leaders and representatives to marketing and development committees and arts boards.
* Think about hospitality as an aspect of your engagement plans. Invite communities to functions, openings, celebrations and launches.
* Add ethnic media to a mix of community, business and grassroots engagement to develop all-powerful word-of-mouth. Develop links with ethnic media journalists and editors. Buy ethno-specific and non-ethno-specific ads.
* Look outside the arts for case studies. Australia's politicians know the power of Australia's political parties, and government service knows the power of ethnic media and multicultural engagement. The telecommunications, banking, health, sports, fast food, supermarket and real-estate industries all use sophisticated multicultural communication strategies – and have serious relationships with a range of ethnic media.

Art and climate justice

Karrina Nolan and Alex Kelly

We are living in a time of rapid global warming and a changing climate: rising sea levels inundating gardens and sacred sites in the Torres Strait; remote communities across northern Australia sweltering through prolonged heat waves; warming seas depleting fish stocks; climate-fuelled bushfires ravaging communities; and floods washing away communities.

Increases in severe weather events such as droughts, cyclones, floods and bushfires are not future possibilities. They are with us now.

Indigenous peoples the world over, who have for millennia shown stewardship, cared for country and protected waters and seas, know we are at a climate tipping point. The way corporations, governments and our economic systems have treated the natural world – as an endless source of resources to be extracted, with little regard for their finite and fragile nature – cannot be sustained.

The stakes could not be higher. We are facing the possibility of an unlivable future, and one that could impact the very fabric of how we live on and are able to connect with country and waters. Our only real choice is transformational change of all of our systems. This includes how we generate energy, grow food, transport goods, make and present our art and cultural projects, as well as how we view and engage with each other.

'The social context of our arts must become more authentically connected to our ethics', says Australian Greens MP and artist Gabrielle de Vietri. 'To the tides of public sentiment. To the urgency of our times. We must interrupt the cultural soliloquy of big business and replace it with the urgent and overwhelming public outcry demanding climate justice.'

Climate justice: Some background

Climate justice is a concept that builds on the groundwork of environmental justice – a term developed to highlight the unfair exposure of poor and marginalised communities (often communities of colour) to environmental hazards, waste and pollution.

The idea of 'environmental justice' came from movements led by People of Colour on Turtle Island (North America), which gained traction through the 1980s and 1990s. Organisers and movements in the Global South (those countries with less developed economies) built on this idea and began to call for climate justice – with the first Climate Justice Summit being held in 2000 alongside the United Nations Conference of Parties (COP) meeting, COP6, in The Hague, and the first official climate justice protest held alongside the COP8 in New Delhi in 2002.

Since then, the term 'climate justice' and the values it speaks to have gained significant traction, influencing the content of the COP meetings and discussions, and framing debates globally, and being taken up by social movements and campaigns around the world.

Like racial justice and disability justice, the term 'climate justice' is now often used to call out the absence of justice. It speaks to all of the ways peoples and communities are largely absent from decision-making that affects them. As international non-government organisation Global Witness explains:

> [Climate justice] recognises that the blame for creating the crisis we find ourselves in is not shared evenly. In an utter travesty of justice, the places which are currently suffering the effects of global warming bear little or no historical responsibility for causing it. Instead, the blame overwhelmingly lies with the rich countries of the Global North which used vast quantities of fossil fuels to power their industrial growth.

Climate justice can also be used to speak to the historic injustice, unequal extraction and financial benefits that have been made from fossil fuels, and the subsequent debt the Global North (countries with more developed and wealthier economies) owes the Global South and, in some cases, make demands for climate reparations (known as 'climate debt').

A climate justice framework

As well as articulating these forms of injustice, climate justice can be a vision for transformative change and used as a framework to approach our work with integrity and build more intersectional approaches into our practice.

This begins by acknowledging the strength and agency of First Nations people on whose country projects are being created. It also means looking to the wisdom and leadership of those most impacted in the community you are working in. Amplifying those with lived experience in shaping the project, decision-making, storytelling and in the public-facing work itself is critical. This means climate justice looks different wherever you are, and should be designed with and by the communities in which you work.

Organisations can take a straightforward approach to climate action by paying attention to who we bank with and where our superannuation is held, as well as reviewing the carbon impacts of touring and presenting work, and considering our travel and transport footprint. There are a range of accessible tools to support these simple steps.

Beyond these infrastructural steps, climate justice–informed practice also backs the agency and expertise of the community it is working with and builds processes that prioritise collaboration, research and responsiveness.

For First Nations communities to be able to represent and speak for themselves, they need to be able to give free and informed prior consent and have self-determination over their land and waterways. This same principle applies to the stories that are shared, the way in which they are made and shared, and the audiences that can access these stories.

Agency and self-determination require that communities have the capacity to say 'Yes' or 'No' to the projects that they want to participate in. For communities to identify what projects they want to say 'Yes' to, they need to be well informed and well connected to each other. They need access to resources, additional experts and information about the impacts of the proposed development on country, the climate, culture and infrastructure.

The arts have a role to play in building space for reflection and connection and other imaginaries, other futures. A connected and cohesive community is fundamental to working collaboratively for change.

Arts projects can bring people together for safe, reflective conversations around big ideas. The arts can also help break down the heaviness of science and policy, allowing space for discussion of fears, hope and other possibilities. We know that a connected and cohesive community is fundamental to working collaboratively for change.

The challenge of climate justice

It is not unusual for individuals, communities or organisations to sometimes want to see climate change through a technological lens and avoid the human rights dimensions of the climate crisis. Or to look away from climate change altogether.

The reality of the science, the scale and complexity of the problem, combined with misinformation and denial, presents a challenge to us all and to artists and arts workers, especially as the concept of climate justice is not yet widely understood or applied in practice. This requires leadership in our words and actions. As Indian writer Amitav Ghosh says:

> When future generations look back they will certainly blame the leaders and politicians of this time for their failures to address the climate crisis. But they may well hold the artists and writers to be equally culpable – for the imagining of possibilities is not, after all, the job of politicians and bureaucrats.

Artists and arts workers are powerfully positioned to drive climate justice. We can do this through our institutional structures, our governance, and the processes through which we make our work, as well as through the narratives and ideas we explore in the art we make.

Of course, climate justice in action is different depending on location and context. It might include paying the rent to Traditional Owners as part of our event ticketing, building informed consent into our creative processes or supporting local regeneration projects. In other places, it may be Aboriginal people self-determining what happens on their country or generating self-owned renewable energy.

Regardless of how it manifests, it's critical for all of us and the protection of country and sacred places that we transition away from fossil fuels. And as we do so, processes that prioritise First Nations leadership, and are grounded in local community agency and control are key. This is self-determination and energy democracy. This is climate justice.

Climate justice everywhere

What does climate justice look like for an arts and cultural project?

Campaigning to protect water or say no to fracking of country might seem a long way from touring a show, rigging lights or promoting an event, but working in a climate-justice-informed way is relevant to every sector.

You may not be installing solar panels or directly campaigning, but you can still work in ways that advance climate justice. Bringing a climate justice lens to making art is not just about the content of the art itself, but the process of making it and the strategies around how it is staged, exhibited or distributed as well as considering who is funding it.

Artwashing

Artwash – a combination of the words 'art' and 'whitewashing' (see also: greenwashing)

The complicity of the arts in providing cover, good publicity, popularity and social licence to fossil-fuel sponsors is increasingly under scrutiny. The practice of fossil-fuel, mining or other private sector companies trying to endear themselves to the public through sponsorship of creative projects and events is understood as 'artwashing'.

Coined by British writer and organiser Mel Evans, 'Artwashing is an extension of the notion of greenwashing, where companies try to make it look like they have green credentials to build credibility for their brand and generate social capital'. Evans asks:

How is it that there is a gap between all these harmful impacts that oil companies like BP have through their daily activities around the world and our acceptance of them as part of our lives? A big part of what happens in that gap is artwash – the way in which oil companies project a better image of themselves to the public through their associations with cultural institutions and sport and their social licence to operate.

'Social license' is the informal cultural acceptance of companies, which is different from the formal agreements they need to operate, such as labour standards or environmental policies. The arts and sports are both so popular and so embedded in our day-to-day lives that they are powerful sponsorship partners for companies that want to remain acceptable to society.

But earlier public pressure has led tobacco and weapons advertising to be banned, and a similar push against fossil-fuel companies is now underway – with a movement calling on the arts to break up with fossil-fuel sponsorship spreading around the world.

Examples include Liberate Tate in the UK, which saw the Tate galleries break ties with BP in 2016. In Australia, Fringe World Perth parted ways with Woodside in 2021 and the Darwin Festival ended their sponsorship agreement with Santos in 2022. In 2023, 350.org and the Climate Council launched the Cut All Ties campaign calling on arts and sports organisations to pledge not to take fossil-fuel money.

These shifts have been in direct response to pressure brought by artists and communities demanding that their beloved arts institutions not be tainted by taking dirty money and instead seek funding elsewhere. Artists and arts organisations are also developing tools to make it easier to take a stance against artwash, including:

- Turtle Island–based Groundwater Arts' #FossilFreeArts pledge
- Boorloo-based pvi collective's Code of Ethics template

- National Association of the Visual Arts (NAVA) Code of Practice, which includes a section on climate adaptation and environmental action.

....

Things to keep in mind

✳ Develop a learning practice. Educate yourself about climate justice. Understanding it is not a one-and-done story; it is an ongoing practice of listening and learning, especially in the unique local contexts in which we are each working. In addition to the resources we've already mentioned, recommended resources include:

- ○ 'First Nations Resistance and Climate Justice' by Karrina Nolan for The Commons Social Change Library
- ○ Original Power principles of self-determination
- ○ Bali Principles of Climate Justice
- ○ Take the Money and Run introduction to *Artwash: Big Oil and the Arts* by UK artist and activist Mel Evans
- ○ 'Bad Romance: Coal, Gas, and Oil Sponsorship in the Australian Arts Industry' commissioned by 350.org and authored by Swinburne University researchers Emma Sherry, Adam Karg, Dan Golding and Olivia Bramley
- ○ 'Maps of Gratitude' by Australian Greens MP and artist Gabrielle de Vietri
- ○ 'Climate Crisis and the Arts: Untangling: Breaking up with Fossil Fuels' with Alex Kelly

and former Australian Greens Senator Scott
Ludlam at Adelaide Writers Week
○ *This Changes Everything: Capitalism Versus the
Climate* by Canadian author and social activist
Naomi Klein
○ 'In the Time of Refuge Collection' by City of
Melbourne through Arts House in partnership
with the Research Unit of Public Cultures,
Melbourne University
○ 'Connections Between Climate Change and
Disability' from Disability and Philanthropy
Forum.

* Rethink your approach based on your learning
practice. Move towards deeper collaboration, co-
design and sharing power on all your projects.
Consent is an ongoing process. Relationships are
everything.
* Listen to the leadership of those with lived
experience. Don't just stop at putting people forward
to talk to the media. Support people to gain the skills
to have agency over their own affairs, including their
involvement with your project.
* Share power. Put your resources and power to the
service of the communities you work in and with.
Elevate the people you work with to positions of
power within your projects and organisations.
* Network with others to build power. Campaigns
that win are based in broad coalitions. Move from
silos to collective organising. You don't have to do
everything – find others on the same road!

* Be bold. We need deep transformative change. Ask and fight for what we need rather than smaller reforms that won't get us to a liberated world.
* Develop ethical sponsorship and ethical partnership frameworks to determine who you will and won't collaborate with, and the principles that will guide those decisions.
* Get out on the streets and support other movements! Join your body with the bodies of others – consider your capacity for protest and direct action.
* Build your plan hand-in-hand with your community. Every community and every project is unique. You can't arrive with a plan; you have to build it together.

Creative practice in disaster recovery

Scotia Monkivitch

Creative recovery uses creative and participatory activities to help people and communities heal from the change and trauma caused by disasters, and reframe lives, landscapes and connections afterwards.

The trauma and loss caused by floods, fires, pandemics or other disasters can severely affect mental health, accessibility and social networks, but traditional approaches to disaster recovery may not be sufficient to address these complex needs. Using arts and culture to respond to crises can offer care and comfort, reduce isolation, increase community cohesiveness and empowerment, and help people safely unpack, reimagine, celebrate or memorialise their experience.

Creative recovery builds new skills and shared optimism, strengthens a sense of place, and creates profound and long-lasting effects through expressing emotions and our understanding of the past, and supporting us to feel hope about the future.

Resilient leaders

Working with crises and disasters means we confront trauma, grief and loss. Trauma-informed practice is a strengths-based framework that acknowledges the profound impact of trauma on people (including ourselves), and promotes physical and emotional safety, trust, empowerment and rebuilding.

Creativity can serve as a catalyst for healing and growth within trauma-informed work. Creative participation activates the prefrontal cortex of our brain, which regulates emotions and impulses. By taking part in creative activities, people and communities can reclaim their identity and authenticity, rebuild neural pathways, and activate healing.

Creative recovery practice is difficult and requires specific learning and skills. Facilitators of creative recovery work must be present, trustworthy, credible, humble and vulnerable, and have skills in cultural competence, analysis, advocacy, collaboration, critical thinking, communication and a passion for lifelong learning.

Creative leaders must understand the broader context of a disaster, think creatively to solve complex problems and relate to traumatised participants. With more and more disasters in an increasingly complex environment, leaders require specific knowledge, creativity, empathy and confidence to provide informed and timely creative support to others through change.

Resilient communities

Creative practitioners foster resilience and recovery after a disaster by creating safe spaces where people can speak and be heard with dignity and respect. Supporting people in telling, developing or interpreting their stories requires time and commitment. A place-based approach that addresses local context, needs and strengths, and responds to locally identified gaps and interests is essential. Collaboration, co-design, shared ownership and accountability are important, along with community engagement, experimentation, fun and action learning.

Climate change and other disasters have a greater impact on people already struggling and can make existing social inequalities worse. Mental health and wellbeing are influenced by existing vulnerabilities in health, access to help and resources, and education. Therefore, creative recovery work should address differences and promote social justice.

Principles for effective creative recovery

To ensure effective creative recovery, integration with broader disaster recovery activities is necessary. Creative practitioners must understand disaster management systems and work safely, respectfully and sustainably within it.

The six National Principles for Disaster Recovery can be used to guide creative recovery practitioners in supporting communities after a crisis:

1   context
2   complexity
3   community-centred approaches
4   coordination
5   communication
6   capacity building.

Context

- Situational awareness and safety: prioritise safety (yourself and others) at all times.

- Interdisciplinary knowledge: develop and share knowledge with other service providers and communities.
- Partnerships: disaster management involves a range of systems and organisations within and outside of affected communities. We can't work in isolation. Flexibility, collaboration and strong communication skills are necessary to navigate the complex issues a crisis leaves behind.
- Shared leadership: it takes time to evolve a responsive, collaborative program with multiple partners. Invest in time for planning for better participation and outcomes.
- Trauma: after a disaster, people, communities, government and service providers will be emotionally and physically exhausted. Take a gentle approach and adjust the pace and scale of your activity to changing needs.

Complexity

- Uniqueness: no two disasters are ever the same. The ways we respond to them should be unique, too.
- Capacity: the growing realities of droughts, fires, floods, storms, pandemics and other disasters stretch resources and capacity on every level. Coordinate with other initiatives to optimise energy and resources.
- Diversity: strong communities are diverse in their activities, strengths, opportunities and people. Provide tailored support that considers social, political and cultural needs.

- Time frames: no individual or community recovers in a linear or specified time frame. Recovery is a long-term journey with evolving needs.
- Problem-solving: creative recovery practitioners need to be skilled problem-solvers and build relationships that promote trust and encourage diverse perspectives and creative problem-solving.
- Critical thinking: critical-thinking skills are essential for understanding the underlying causes of community challenges and inequalities, and for working towards positive change. Challenge approaches that marginalise people or groups or perpetuate false information.

Community-centred approaches

- Targeted focus: creative recovery efforts should be tailored for a specific community to make sure those affected by a disaster can actively participate in their own recovery.
- Recognising local knowledge: local creative practitioners know their communities best and have existing work and personal relationships. Investment in local skills development ensures an ongoing legacy.
- Ethics and cultural competence: responsible and respectful creative recovery requires ethical reasoning and cultural competence, self-reflection and openness to guidance and feedback.

Coordination

- Transparency: clear and accountable project management is crucial in managing interpersonal relationships, resolving conflict, and efficiently managing shifting priorities to ensure needs are met.
- Learning: the multi-disciplinary and changing nature of this field means continuous professional development is necessary.
- Flexibility: creative recovery approaches require us to be open to cooperation and compromise, adapt to specific issues, and create meaningful experiences that resonate with a community's values and context.

Communication

- Language: the languages we use are crucial in building connection and rapport. Practitioners should have skills in reliable and approachable communication techniques.
- Listening: actively attune to the needs, concerns and aspirations of community members. Support the development of responsive, self-determined activities that link localised issues and visions to broader climate justice movements and build new collective narratives for resilience and hopeful futures.
- Empathy: creative-recovery practitioners need to possess sensitivity and empathy towards the experiences and emotions of those impacted by the disaster.
- Wellbeing: we need to prioritise self-care in order to be able to keep doing this work, including accessing professional support.

Capacity building

- A long-term view: recovery is a long journey. Creative recovery programs need to grow legacy, future preparedness and long-term community resilience.

Creative recovery activities

Creative recovery projects will differ in scope, complexity and in the roles required of the creative practitioner, depending on the nature of the disaster, the needs of the community, available resources, and the expertise of the artists and organisations involved.

They often start by exploring non-arts issues with community participants and stakeholders, and then collaborating on a creative response. Workshops, training programs and skill-sharing initiatives can build the artistic and creative capacity of individuals and help them become active participants in the recovery process. Projects may involve:

- murals, sculptures or installations that reflect the resilience and spirit of the community, while rebuilding a sense of place and identity
- visual and performing arts projects that encourage the expression of emotions or offer respite, self-expression and community bonding
- eco-art installations that raise awareness about environmental issues and promote sustainable recovery practices
- new community rituals, festivals or ceremonies to make collective meaning of an experience and imagine a shared future

- performance projects that raise the awareness of disaster impacts on marginalised members of the community
- writing projects that share a community's stories and visions for the future.

···

Things to keep in mind

As every situation is different, it's not possible to directly apply a single model to every disaster. Instead, we need to learn about the common and unique impacts of each disaster and community and develop a program that responds to and respects their specific needs.

There are, however, some critical factors common to all successful creative recovery programs:

∗ Involvement of communities in decision-making is crucial.

∗ Remember that everyone is overwhelmed. Minimise imposition on communities and services during consultation, and support shared resource development.

∗ Provide resources to support community members to take part, such as language translations, transport or childcare.

∗ Recognise that different people will be at different stages of recovery and that grief is different for everybody. Projects need to hold space for people who just need a cup of tea to those who are bursting to activate and drive change.

∗ Ensure a sense of safety and security in high-needs settings, such as schools.

＊ Connect to and support existing initiatives and resources.

＊ Incorporate principles for good mental health and work with mental health support colleagues. Enable time, rest, reflection and broader relationships for ongoing support beyond your program.

＊ Work through reflective processes with leadership by and collaboration with diverse and marginalised community members.

＊ Take care of yourself. While we can't fully prepare for what we encounter during a disaster, psychological preparedness and peer support can help us cope with the stress during and after disasters.

Reworlding: Adapting to the climate emergency through relationality

Jen Rae and Claire G. Coleman

We live in a period of un-ness: ours is a time of the unprecedented, unexpected, uncertain, unstable, unpredictable, unknowable and unimaginable as global warming inches closer to 1.5°C where the impacts of climate change will increase dramatically in intensity and frequency.

The climate emergency is humanity's greatest threat and challenge. Climate change will affect every aspect of our lives and the resources that support our wellbeing. This means that we are now in the 'adaptation emergency' requiring a rapid and profound reorganising of all things.

Therefore, it is critical to untether from our conventional ways of working across and within institutional structures, and collaborate better by deepening and sustaining relationships beyond projects, transactions and funding cycles. Importantly, we also need to amplify the capacities and voices of those less represented in climate and other disaster-related emergencies – as well as consider and act for those who are yet to be born.

Transformational change and resilience will require a radical reorganisation of our functional and relational systems and the embedding of long-view thinking that prioritises justice between generations. Critical to this process is acknowledgment and accountability, knowledge transmission and navigating complexity with communities – firmly holding urgency in one hand and relationality in the other.

We begin reworlding in the 'everywhen'

Indigenous worldviews centre relationships (what we call 'relationality'). Our ways don't just connect people but also include non-human relations and places, over all space and all time. Our ways of understanding, sharing and receiving knowledge engage with how knowledge is obtained and attributed. In this way, storylines are bound, authenticated and held by many – ensuring accountability and longevity.

Reworlding combines three Indigenous concepts – rematriation, reconciliation and resurgence.

- Rematriation is an Indigenous way of life that recentres respect, restoration and care for Mother Earth. It means we maintain our kinship with each other and with all life forms.
- Reconciliation centres repair, healing and making amends for past and present colonial injustices. It means we establish equitable and respectful relationships for the future.
- Resurgence is about reclamation, renewal and revival. It means we honour our ancestral legacies and reconnect storylines.

These come from Indigenous futuring (complex ways of thinking about the future) and survivance relationships (survival and resistance). We lean into the tensions between their Indigenous and non-Indigenous use.

Reworlding exists in the 'everywhen', a deep time/timeless/non-time named by Australian anthropologist WEH Stanner that says the past, present and future all coexist in the eternal now. The past affects our present, but so does our future. Imagining the future changes our actions in the present, and thus changes the future, too.

Métis Elder Maria Campbell explained how artists and writers are the mirrors that show people what our world could be. This includes what should have been if colonisation never happened. Colonialism can then be understood as a mere blip in time (albeit one with catastrophic consequences).

Therefore, when we approach reworlding through speculative futuring, protocols and/or ceremony, we decolonise and Indigenise the future. This can disrupt the Western emphasis on competition between individuals, exploitation and extractive ways of thinking and participation. Feelings of inertia and scarcity can give way to abundance and gratitude.

Relational accountability

Dismantling colonial systems and advocating for change needs a diversity of approaches and an investment into collective knowledge sharing (not 'reinventing the wheel').

Accountability is pivotal at both a grassroots level and institutionally. It requires deep collaboration to combine all our resources, skills, knowledge and capacities to ensure a liveable future for future ancestors, amplify impact and adapt to rapidly changing conditions.

Knowledge circles

We do this work in collaboration with others or in 'knowledge circles' (also called 'yarning' or 'talking' circles). The circle is an Indigenised approach, a working space in which all are equal and consensus is sought. Knowledge circles are built on generosity and a sense that all contributions to the circle deserve respect.

The circle in which knowledge is generated is as important as the information itself. Respecting the relationships that led to the development of that knowledge is essential.

Knowledge created in the circle belongs to the circle and should be attributed as such. Taking information out of a circle or group without acknowledgment is a form of appropriation that is often ignored. It is unethical, but not uncommon, for people to claim knowledge from a group and branch out on their own to exploit that knowledge for individual gain.

The best practice is to 'take the circle with us'. Invite people from the circle or group to collaborate in future projects that use the knowledge they collectively developed. A practical application of this within community-engaged practice is engaging ethically with the cultural intellectual property of collaborators by acknowledging their role, contribution and context of the knowledge transmission. This is how we foster coalitions, care and the amplification of each other's practices and voices.

This will require new ways of thinking, relating and learning collectively across cultural divides and timescales, including learnings that come from (and belong to) the cultural context in which they are developed, and including knowledge systems connected to a person's creative and/or cultural practices, their ancestral lands and/or the context of a group or event.

Asking contributors how they want to be acknowledged is a good way to ensure people are given credit for their generosity and insights. This could be a community-engagement workshop, an artist-led socially engaged project or co-design process. Respectful acknowledgment recognises that each person is an expert at something and offers contributors rightful acknowledgment and, in some cases, copyright.

The responsibility to not steal or appropriate the stories or contribution of others lies with the artist or practitioner, recorder and/or transmitter of the knowledge. When collecting knowledge from someone (such as an oral history), it is important to keep a record of its ownership. In many cases, this may require contracts and protocols that offer protection and cultivate trust in collaborative activities and ensure knowledge keepers maintain copyright.

Using protocols

When we have relational accountability, we are invited to be our best selves. Protocols are ethical principles that guide the behaviour we need to do so. They vary between different Indigenous cultural groups, and have also become more common in non-Indigenous activities.

In First Peoples contexts, protocols are designed to protect the cultural and intellectual property rights of knowledge keepers and guide the conduct of others in a meaningful and respectful manner. Protocols help ensure cultural safety, clarify roles, determine processes for communication and act on breaches. They foster understanding of the value of what is being learnt and how it came into being.

As the long emergency of climate change unfolds, we will be put through many tests that challenge us individually and collectively. It will ask us questions for which we might not have answers. Our greatest hope is that the answers lie within our relationships – past, present and those we cultivate into the future. Now is the time to connect, collaborate and amplify.

Our future generations are counting on us.

Things to keep in mind

The following protocols guide all the workshops and activities of the Centre for Reworlding, ensuring respectful and mindful engagement with all collaborators and participants. They were developed in a workshop with Aunties Vicki Couzens, Brownyn Razem, Vicki Kinai and Muhubo Sulieman for the First Assembly for the Centre for Reworlding and Portage project at Arts House in 2021.

✻ Let questions do the heavy lifting. You will be rewarded for your curiosity, generosity and reciprocity.

* Be mindful of the energy you give and the energy you take. Listen to each other with the same passion and respect you want (don't hog the ball, for example, or toss it out of the circle).
* Understand that everyone is an expert at something. This may include their knowledge, generational perspective, different cultural understanding or lived experience.
* Lean into the tensions. We are all learning how to become comfortable with the uncomfortable.
* First impressions shift when you have informed judgment. Listen. Respond instead of reacting.
* Try to be objective and acknowledge your biases.
* Don't worry about being right, having the 'right' language, solving the problem or having all the answers.
* Exist in this space in ways that are most comfortable for you. Understand that everyone exists in spaces in different ways, and how someone can best engage and listen might look different from how you do.
* Acknowledge and honour the contributions of others inside the circle when you leave. Acknowledgment of the contributions of others is pivotal to the development and maintenance of the relationships within the Centre and with collaborators.

Squads and swarms: Engaging with communities online

Seb Chan

Much has changed in the 30+ years since Australians started connecting and communicating online. Some of us might remember using phrases like 'logging on' or 'getting online' to describe the physical experience of 'connecting to the internet'. In the pre-smartphone era, this perpetuated a common notion of 'digital dualism' – a belief that the digital world is 'virtual' and the physical world (more) 'real', This notion still pervades popular media discussions of the internet and digital cultures. But any sense of divide between 'real' and digital life disappeared with the rapid emergence of the smartphone. By the early 2010s, the majority of the population was persistently online (whether we were aware of it or not).

Micro communities

Organisations still using this binary approach could benefit from thinking about online communities in a more nuanced and segmented way – as smaller, overlapping communities of identity, interest, geography or more.

One of the key things to understand is that who you may perceive you are communicating with may not be obvious, and that people have multiple identities and present those identities in different ways.

What is different in an online environment is that those multiple identities can not only be expressed in a different context, but also across multiple platforms, and in many cases also be pseudo-anonymous or anonymous. How many and exactly who you are interacting with at any particular time may be unclear, or even unknowable.

Knowing how micro communities function online is no different from any other subculture – it takes time to learn their platforms, language and subtext. Figuring out the actual size and scale of the community you're working with is part of the process – as well as realising that those you see or hear may not represent the full size and nature of the group. Meaning and understanding is created through the process of being within that community.

Squads and swarms

The speed of change of the digital space is very challenging for traditional social movements that are inherently slow, which is why we find behavioural practices like squads and swarms online.

The notion of 'squads' initially comes from multiplayer video-gaming communities where it was used to describe the behaviours of people coming together online for a particular 'quest' or mission. As our social, political and community lives have become increasingly lived on and through digital platforms, this squad behaviour has become much more commonplace and squads now can form around any common purpose, activity or task.

These temporary squads don't necessarily share values or even a common sense of meaning, but can be very powerful (from the flash mobs of the early 2000s to rapid contemporary micro protests) – able to quickly gather, form and then disperse. Like in the video games that they emerged from, each squad's social bonds are very much task-oriented and usually time-limited.

'Swarms' are another form of online behaviour that the scale and speed of digital platforms enable. Connected to particular identities, interests or fandoms, large numbers of online accounts can swarm around people or conversations to push an agenda. In the late 20th century, we saw early popular non-digital media forms of this in 'culture jamming' of advertising campaigns, street postering, and through 'tactical media'; however, this now takes place much more visibly, unpredictably and much faster on digital platforms. One meme or post can be circulated, remixed, parodied and shamed by millions in quick time.

Squads and swarms are effective because other traditional forms are unable to adapt to the speed that digital work and communication require. As organisations and practitioners wanting to engage with online communities, we need to remember that these happen organically and form in unpredictable ways, which makes them hard to control, particularly over the long term.

There are many ethical concerns to be considered – the formation of squads and swarming behaviours are also the tools of online bullying and the spread of both unintentional and intentional dis/misinformation. It is important to be aware that since the 2010s and the mass consolidation of digital platforms, these behaviours are now a core feature of the contemporary online environment.

There are many squads and there are many swarms happening at any moment in time – if you are 'extremely online', you may already be part of some without knowing it. We need to meet people where they are, not expect them to come to us. This means we need to find out what motivates the actual people at the end of their virtual identities. The process of becoming part of a digital community is part of doing this sort of community-engaged work.

Online in real time

In the digital space, we use both synchronous (real-time video chats or multiplayer games) and asynchronous communication tools (email, newsletters, blogs or message boards). Using synchronous, face-to-face elements in digital projects reduces the risk of misinterpretation and miscommunication, and builds a sense of community and trust, but it also limits speed, reach and scale.

Although the popular idea of the internet is of being 'global', the reach and scale of being online in real time is all about time zones. Working digitally may give us asynchronous access to the world, but it may be more helpful to think of the globe in vertical strips of time zones to get a more realistic sense of who we're likely to reach in real time.

Digital inequality and safety

While the pandemic took even more of us online, it also highlighted significant inequalities in terms of access to and the quality of online communication, as well as data speed and digital literacy. It also reinforced an illusion that everyone was online, when in fact they weren't (two million Australians still don't have affordable access to the internet at all, and others lack the skills or technology to access it fully).

During the pandemic, digital communities provided connection. Unfortunately, building a new sense of community solely through communicating online without a balance of face-to-face interactions also created a ripe environment for misinformation and exploitation of people with low digital literacy and exacerbated existing digital exclusion.

Digital-native work

Digital communities aren't just consultation participants or audiences. They're also teeming with creatives and artists with whom we can create new work online.

The ideas and artistic projects that work best are native to the platforms and processes of the digital world. Rather than trying to move our existing programs online, we need to understand what digital-native work is – work that can only be done on and through digital platforms, which may be quite different from the type and nature of the work that is done face-to-face.

We need to take care to create safe and equitable online spaces – be that through agreeing on ways to behave towards each other online (to reduce the risk of lurkers or trolls) or creating private, ephemeral or evaporating projects (that don't leave digital traces that participants might not want to follow them into the future).

Is there a post-digital world?

In this 'post'-pandemic space, we've seen a lot of organisations drop their digital projects and communities. It's easy to see the challenges of rapidly changing technology and communication behaviours as something that's just too hard.

But the reality now is that even those we previously engaged with face-to-face also have digital personas and communities, which they are increasingly comfortable being part of. Many disabled and regional people got access to types of cultural experiences for the first time. New opportunities were created, new social relations were formed, and many simple accessibility measures were implemented – most notably the normalisation and expectation of open captioning on video content. With city/suburb/regional divides changing as working-from-home has become accepted in some industries, people who were previously excluded from engaging with creative and community activities by time or caring responsibilities have greater access.

We cannot go back. There is only going forward into a new, hybrid model. That means any digital community-building is not an add-on – it is the work. The community has changed, and that means digital is no longer optional. Short of a global infrastructure collapse, the digital aspect of our lives is not going away.

....

Things to keep in mind

No-one can be really well versed in the rapidly changing nuances of digital work and communication these days. In a field that moves faster than this book can be published, there are no canonical 'top tips'. So what can we do?

* Slow down, watch, look and listen to the communities that you are a part of.
* Instability is absolutely key to understanding online communities. There is no fixedness.
* Technology will continue to change and people, if given time and the space to explore each new digital tool, will come to use them in interesting and unexpected ways.
* Acknowledge that digital inequality exists, and work with groups and organisations to address the lowest levels of access to physical equipment and connectivity.
* Use tools like the Australian Digital Inclusion Index to respond to the different barriers of access across our broader communities (including financial barriers).

....

#EpicFail

Jade Lillie

We all fail – as individuals, as groups and collectives, as organisations, and as sectors. Sometimes, these failures can be serious and significant. Sometimes, we make mistakes that we, or our project, can't come back from – I categorise these as an #EpicFail.

You may have burned an important relationship, misstepped on a cultural issue or made promises you cannot keep. These moments are big (hard) learning opportunities and mistakes we really should avoid making again.

The problem with an 'epic fail' in community-engaged contexts is that they tend to be quite public. They can impact someone's experience of a project or organisation and their experience of the artists or communities involved. That's why epic fails in community-engaged experiences sometimes feel exposing, monumental and ... epic.

Often, we frame these failures as 'things we can do better', softening the language to make it more palatable. But doing so doesn't always allow us to grow or take responsibility and own the things we haven't done well.

An #EpicFail should be something we can share – something we can talk about, learn from and reflect upon together. We can then use this as an opportunity to do things differently in the future. As practitioners, collaborators, facilitators and leaders, we need to be able to have these conversations. While they're not always easy (particularly when they involve personal mistakes), we all grow from having these conversations and looking at the ways we could do better.

Why we fail

The key reasons practitioners and projects fail:

- Communication. This could include a lack of communication between partners and stakeholders, or differences in the ways they communicate. This is the main way people and projects fail to deliver. Clear and transparent communication isn't always easy, but it is important. Even if there are multiple agendas at play and you don't wish to share every detail with everyone involved, always answer questions and be as transparent as possible about the work you are doing together.
- Ego. When ego overrides the values of a project or personalities override the purpose, the most important thing is to focus on the work. What is the best outcome for the work? What is the best path forward for the work?
- Complacency. If you are in the implementation phase, it is essential to make sure you're on top of the details. This means consistency, care and clarification. Forget these things and the wheels start to come off.

- Forced engagement. When you've received funding for a project and the circumstances have changed, don't force it. You are better off giving the money back than forcing an outcome that is not aligning with the community context, timing or people needed to make it happen. Simply, do not do it.
- Too many cooks. Being a collective is one thing but a lack of clarity about who to come to with information or concerns is a problem. Who is looking after communications with the community and how can people get in touch? Ideally, there should be a door where people can show up. (This is why organisations tend to have more success in long-term engagement with communities.)
- Flexibility. Being clear about the negotiable and non-negotiable aspects of a project is critical to success. This also allows for flexibility and transparency about when this is possible. Too often, the idea and concept have already been locked in before the start of a project, which leads to a lack of ability or willingness to negotiate with stakeholders or to adapt along the way. Flexibility is your best friend when it comes to working in community contexts.

Failing in leadership

Being a great 'leader' is sometimes confused with 'having all the answers' – this is not possible.

In leadership, often we are asked to respond to problems that need fixing. This can mean we rarely talk about our own epic fails in a meaningful and honest way. But failing to do so can erode trust in us as leaders (or in the organisations we represent). In these instances, try to focus on the work rather than the personal, and once you have expressed your concerns or feedback, let it go. Always come back to the work, the goal or objective – the reason you started this in the first place. When possible, try navigating any issues by centring the work, rather than personalities or personal preferences.

It is important to approach failure with an open mind, without judgment until all sides of a problem or a situation are clear. Try to remember that all people make mistakes and it is more rare than common for someone to actively undermine or aim to damage their co-workers or collaborators.

Leadership comes at all levels. In community-engaged contexts, 'the leaders' are rarely the people at the 'top' of the organisation. Communities, partners and collaborators will all have self-identified leaders. Step out of the hierarchy and meet people with the view that you are all leading the process and experience together.

The experimental epic fail

Community-engaged practice is often a deeply experimental practice. This doesn't necessarily mean that we experiment within our projects, but that true community-engaged work needs to combine a set of relationships, dynamics and moment-in-time experiences that come together to form a fuller picture.

This, in its true essence, can be considered an experimental act – in the same way that a scientist may undertake an 'experiment' that results in failure, success or the creation of an entirely new and unexpected thing.

Facilitators of community-engaged experiences can understand projects in the same way – as well-structured, safe and experimental approaches to social, cultural or political issues that use arts and culture as their primary tools (in which failure may be as valid an outcome as success).

Giving people an opportunity to correct a situation is an important part of developing relationships. But in an online world where things are 'called out' more than they are celebrated, in a practice that is not really encouraged to learn and fail, how do we have open conversations about the challenges and failures when working in community-engaged contexts?

Rather than accusing someone of doing the 'wrong' thing, perhaps provide some feedback, share your own insights (calmly and respectfully) and then ask ... how can I help?

Embracing the #EpicFail

Failures are part of the work we do. They may become less prevalent as we become more experienced, or they change and sometimes the stakes are higher. We may become more familiar with crossroad moments and the ways that things can fail. We do our best to not make the same mistakes. But failure is unavoidable.

Often, the issues are more about relationships not working, miscommunications or timing than the logistics of a project themselves. Failure is part of the process. We learn the most from the times we make the greatest mistakes. We know we've learnt from them when we can talk about them as key moments in our careers; when we practise the lessons that have stayed with us through the projects we went on to do; and in how we use that learning to build conversations about the #EpicFail into our work:

- Start early. As part of idea/concept development, include a section on the ways you might fail. In addition to a risk assessment, this could be the thing that kicks off a conversation between collaborators, artists, producers and communities about the ways that we might fail.
- Know ourselves. We can ask ourselves about our strengths and weaknesses, and make those clear in our collaborating teams. For example, if you know you are not great at the 'finishing' part of a project, make sure there is another person on the 'finishing' stage in order to stay connected all the way to the end.
- Share the stories. When debriefing a project or an idea, share all of the parts of the process. Include the things we did right as well as the things we managed to get wrong and would not do again.
- Do not pretend. There are words and phrases we use to convince everyone that everything about that project was a success. We've all done it. Wouldn't it be refreshing to talk about the things we failed at and learnt from? Sure, we all learn from the good things,

but we learn more from the not-so-good things because who wants to recreate these?

Given the chance, collaborators and communities will welcome the honesty and transparency of these conversations.

Things to keep in mind

* Develop relationships in a way that allows you to be honest and share the struggles of a project with your collaborators.
* Make decisions about the work rather than the personalities or politics of a project.
* Try not to lock the door shut or burn a bridge when it comes to relationships – you never know when you will be sitting across from that person or community again. It is important that you have closure on the last project before being faced with an awkward conversation about the next one.
* When things go wrong, take responsibility for the things that are yours. It is important to acknowledge when things haven't gone well. It is OK to say sorry.
* Commit to learning from and sharing your mistakes.
* Debrief with someone who is kind and has some experience in your setting.
* Write about your failure. Where did you go wrong? What do you want to remember for next time?
* Don't try to be perfect – it is a trap!
* Be kind to yourself through your failures.
* Start clear, stay clear and finish clear.

A duty of care

Kate Larsen

What we do (or choose not to do) affects other people.
We all have a duty to care for the safety and wellbeing of
the people and communities we work alongside. A legal,
logistical and ethical issue, duty of care is sometimes
called the 'neighbour principle', which means we all have
a responsibility to those around us.

When we're leading a project or running an
organisation, that duty goes beyond the personal.
Employers, board members and project leaders have a
duty of care to create a safe environment for our teams.
Artists, employees and independent practitioners have a
duty to the organisations we work for, but also to respect
and look out for each other. And everyone has a duty to
care for our participants, the communities we work with,
and ourselves.

Why is it important?

Legally, duty of care is a common-law principle most
often found in occupational health and safety or
negligence legislation. Getting it wrong can get you
in big trouble – such as if there is an accident or injury
(or worse) because your crew did not have the right
safety equipment.

Duty of care is operationally important for our
organisations and projects, as well as for the success

and integrity of the work that we make. Not taking care of the rifts and relationships in a community performance, for example, could mean no-one takes the stage on opening night.

Since the pandemic, meeting this duty of care has become even more urgent and important. Unfortunately, at a time when we needed more from our leaders, we saw many step back instead of up. This is understandable, considering nobody was their best selves – but our duty of care is enhanced during times of crisis, not diminished, and it will take time to rebuild the relationships and trust that the experience stripped from our projects, workplaces and relationships.

Doing our duty

Essentially, duty of care asks us to anticipate and act on anything that could be 'reasonably foreseen' to cause harm – whether that's through poor planning, neglect, risky behaviour or oversight. We can do our duty in a range of different ways: from making sure the right people are involved in a project and that we have the right contracts, processes and insurances in place, to the informal ways we check in with our partners and participants.

Ask yourself questions like these at the start, middle and end of your projects:

- How accessible is my location? How can I make sure everyone has a say (especially if they don't speak the same language or communicate in the same way)?
- How can I create a culturally, emotionally and psychologically safe space? Does my team have the

right safety checks and experience? Has everyone agreed to a code of conduct?

- What are the risks if I do X? What are the risks if I don't do Y? How do I plan for the risks I can't control?

Duty of care to communities

Being able to participate, feeling respected and valued, and having access to opportunities are central to wellbeing. But the way we make this happen isn't static. One size doesn't fit all. Our duty of care changes with each project and each community, depending on the level of risk involved and the vulnerabilities of the people we're working with.

In community-engaged practice, the first step – always – is to listen. Make sure to set up a way of working that is open, inclusive and led by the community itself. Be clear, collaborative and thoughtful. Be flexible when plans evolve or change. Keep checking in.

Know when to step up, but when to shut up too – particularly if you're working with a community or issue of which you don't personally have lived experience. Leadership can also be shown in making the choice not to lead, to not be the first or the only one to speak, or to not be the one making the final decisions.

Duty of care to organisations, boards and committees

Australia's not-for-profit governance model is problematic in many ways. Many governance processes are exclusionary and non-inclusive, which means boards and committees often don't reflect the communities they're set up to represent.

How boards and committees meet their duty of care to their people is another common problem, ranging from the (usually too high) workload they require to service their (usually too frequent) meetings, to how present (or absent) members are in an organisation, or how they communicate, as well as the wellbeing of individual members and the effectiveness of boards as a whole.

Committees and boards can do better, starting by clarifying the difference between what you think you need to do (and how), what your legislation and funders require, and what your organisation and people actually need. Redefine a governance ecology that works for you. Implement reviews and recruitment targets to make sure your decision-makers are skilled and representative. Reduce your reporting and meeting frequency and provide more ways for people to attend them. Ask how you can help. Trust your team to do their jobs.

Duty of care to ourselves

In spite of its many rewards, not-for-profit work is a constant and exhausting challenge: perpetually under-resourced and propped up by passionate people better at looking after other people's needs than our own, often to our detriment – financially, physically and emotionally.

'Post'-pandemic, this appetite is finally starting to change, along with an understanding that self-care isn't selfish, it's vital – not only for individuals, but also for our communities. If we burn out, they miss out. So, don't be embarrassed by how you feel or what you need. Set boundaries and protect them. Give yourself a break.

Protocols for research, consultation and writing

We often think about community-engaged practice in terms of projects or initiatives with or for particular groups, but we need to apply the same principles to research, writing and policy development about them, too.

For example, if you research an article on disability arts without interviewing disabled artists or yourself identifying as a disabled person, you risk unfairly representing or damaging the reputation of that community. If you consult with children without following appropriate protocols, you risk damaging community members or their families. If a non-Indigenous Australian writes historical fiction from the point of view of a First Nations character, with only two-dimensional stereotypes or without First Nations characters at all, they risk compounding the experience of colonialism as well as not being taken seriously for their work.

Ask yourself: who is best positioned to tell a particular story or undertake a particular piece of research, writing or policy work? If it's not you, can you pass on the opportunity or platform someone else, or bring them into the team? How can you get the information or permission you need from people with direct lived experience (and more than just one)? Are you willing to listen, change or stop what you're doing based on the advice you receive? How will you credit or compensate people for their wisdom and time?

Check the protocols on the Creative Australia website to help consult with communities in ways that encourage respect, self-determination and care.

Failing our duty

Duty of care can be complex and daunting. Getting it right takes time. Getting it wrong takes no time at all, but can have a long-lasting impact. In legal terms, this is where negligence can be said to occur: when something you do (or choose not to do) leads to someone being harmed.

A physically unsafe environment can easily result in injury. A toxic work culture can lead to bullying or burnout. Fly-in-fly-out funding-dependent projects can lead to rushed, disappointing outcomes and cynical, damaged relationships.

Failure of duty of care is dangerous. People can get hurt. Communities can be put in conflict, or be so disillusioned that they don't engage again. You can damage your own reputation and that of the sector. Your project may have to suddenly change or stop. Make sure to discuss contingency plans with communities from the start of each project, and make changes and cancellation plans in consultation with them, too.

Things to keep in mind

* Listen. Make sure you know what a community wants from the project and how they want to get there. Keep checking in.
* Anticipate. Plan. Be prepared. Identify and manage risks. Make sure to budget for access and contingency costs.
* Act. Don't wait for things to get better. Do something about it. Doing nothing is not an option. Doing nothing is a failure of your duty of care.
* Be clear. Be consistent. Protect yourself and the people you work with by writing everything down.
* Be flexible. Things are going to change. Deal with those changes calmly and with good humour.
* Acknowledge your mistakes. Intentions count less than how something is received. Hurt or offence caused accidentally still hurts. Be accountable when things go wrong. Acknowledge, apologise and ask how best to move on.
* Celebrate your successes. Make sure celebratory moments work for everybody involved.
* Model good practice. If you don't take care of yourself, how can you expect others to do so?
* Don't panic. No person or project is perfect. No-one can plan for everything that can go wrong. But it's important to try, do our best, and to own and learn from our mistakes.

No end date: Time frames and expectations

Paschal Berry

The arts sector is a beautiful beast: capable of great feats and spectacular failures. At our best, artists, arts workers, producers and curators who work in communities can inspire important cultural shifts that impact future generations. But at our worst, we can develop into creatures that rampage across social and cultural landscapes – and not know when to leave.

One of our biggest failures in community-engaged practice is not finding the time to sit with communities to dream up a realistic timeline and exit strategy. Our presence in a community must be based on the idea that our relationship with the people who live there needs to evolve. We need to know when we are no longer needed.

We can be part of the problem

Often, we are approached by project partners with the idea that we can solve social challenges through the scope of a project, that what we do together can 'fix' something within a community.

Often, we begin a project by taking an opportunity to apply for funding – often framed as a strategic initiative that then disappears and is never offered again.

Often, we are armed with short project timelines and limited resources.

And often, we preference the artist's process and the time they need to create good work – sometimes over the needs of the community.

As leaders of these failed experiments, we can leave locals feeling empty and used. We can even drive those residents out – after making their neighbourhoods so desirable they can no longer afford to live in them. The last thing communities need is for artists and arts workers to replicate the failures of community services or government, or the continued shaming of these communities through mainstream media.

Attempting a meaningful collaboration based on the resources attached to a single project is counter-intuitive. It doesn't create meaningful and transparent relationships with communities, and it means that projects are only resourced short-term. It is these encounters where ethics has to play a role – in navigating the inherent tension and power dynamics between participants and artists (the locals and the tourists) – and in accepting that we might be part of the problem.

We can be part of the solution

We need to critique our presence in communities, to be aware of the space and time that we take up, and avoid causing harm.

The most successful projects encourage collaboration across sectors. As artists and arts workers, it is our job to be intermediaries between the community and the people who have the power to solve things. It's about reclaiming the democratic space that activates direct contact between community leaders and public servants.

Working in dysfunctional communities and spaces, there is a lot of weariness on both sides of the divide. In the end, people need someone to listen and take action. Rigorous and strategic planning allows us to match the most productive person of power to the most effective community leader.

Working with partners, such as local governments, is one way to make sure projects have an afterlife. It also provides an organisational infrastructure that remains after the funding period, and which has the capacity to sustain and reignite local interest. Local government arts centres should open the door to other sections of their councils. Chances are, different departments already work with artists, either through events, public art, community development or as consultants in urban planning projects.

To end well, we have to start well

A community comes to you with a proposal to work together (or you start to build a relationship with a community yourself). What next?

Make sure you consider if your project proposal has enough resources to deliver within a realistic time frame. Think about what kind of time you need to prepare and deliver a project. It is important to create conditions for maximum participation of key community stakeholders (such as First Nations Elders, teachers from local schools, cultural groups, church groups or local businesses).

Make the first community meeting count. And ensure that the meeting is the very first key date of your project.

Ask the community what they want to achieve from the collaboration. Using those objectives as a guide, create a realistic timeline that includes regular evaluation of the project and a plan for how you will hand leadership of the project back to the community, and provide the community with opportunities to gain personal and professional development through your networks. And make sure you have a clear exit strategy that suits all parties.

The artistic process should be the catalyst to creating an infrastructure of support that encourages community members to enact real change in their communities.

Approaching the end

An exit strategy, like any deadline, gives you a sense of immediacy and responsibility. It's important to build schedules that have clear delivery dates based on mutually beneficial goals. For example:

- Does the community have direct access to individuals who are able to help?
  - » key personnel from all tiers of government (council departments; state departments; federal MPs, etc.)
  - » key personnel from local businesses, education sector, community organisation
  - » key personnel from major cultural institutions (smaller and more grassroots projects are often catalysts to bigger community-led collaborations).
- Do these individuals value the project enough to embed it within the culture of their organisation?

- » Sustainable practice can't rely on personal interests or the passion of an individual.
  If the engagement is with council personnel, their entire department must be engaged for continuity.
- » An infrastructure of community support connects local organisations, community groups and local businesses to the wider arts and cultural landscape.
- Who is taking the lead locally?
  - » An exit strategy should consider the development of local artists, arts workers, curators and producers to take over.
  - » Form an enclave of community leaders, across diverse ages, lived experience and cultural representation.
  - » Establish regular community meetings led by local leaders and representation from diverse local stakeholders.

When we get it wrong, it can be like a theatre company that lives forever but that no longer communicates to the audience they were set up to engage. Far worse, it can create a stagnant culture that promotes co-dependent behaviour. This is where a project tries to find relevance by constantly chasing funding opportunities, often reactively, while never being critical of its impact on the locals who must deliver it.

Importantly, an exit doesn't mean an end or abandonment of the real relationships you've formed with individuals and the community at large. We can remain useful beyond the exit date.

Find sustainable ways of retaining connections, such as connecting people to opportunities that might arise from your networks – professional pathways for young people, funding opportunities, sharing information about exemplary community projects, or linking people to other communities that encourage global exchanges.

....

Things to keep in mind

* Clearly map out your long-term schedule for working with a community.
  * Is the project structure clear?
  * Who is leading the project?
  * Do all project partners understand their part?
  * What are the key pathways for the community?
  * What are the opportunities for young people?
  * What are the opportunities for intergenerational personal and professional development?
* Think about what resources you are allocating to the project (time, funding, in-kind support, etc.) and what you will use to measure the success of this investment. Honesty about financial and in-kind contributions allows for realistic and strategic discussions about the future of working together.
* Be transparent about your resources. This allows your collaborators to understand end dates and to manage expectations.
* Revisit your aims and objectives regularly, and have rigorous conversations about what else is left to achieve. If mutually agreeable, set a new timeline that can meet your objective.

* Integrate personal and professional development of local community members into the project. Make sure they are involved in everything from fundraising to negotiating spaces, or seeking opportunities with government and private entities.
* Work towards a final event or public outcome that becomes the symbolic handover of the project to local leaders, producers and/or community workers.
* With the community, evaluate the success and challenges of the first year of working together. Create an honest climate for appraising projects. Be brave enough to hear what is hard to hear. Maybe, you are not needed here.
* Retain contact but give up project leadership. (Unless, of course, the community is asking you to stay).

Culturally safe evaluation

Timoci O'Connor

In the wake of the COVID-19 pandemic, government funding and distribution of spending has increased on highly controlled programs and interventions within community settings. These initiatives hold the promise of reconstruction and rebuilding, with compliance requirements to account for how/where the funding is used. But hidden within the seemingly worthy goal of evaluation for accountability, lies a shadow of colonial intentions and agendas – compliance measures that disempower communities to self-determine their own priorities, stigmatise their capacity to manage their own affairs, divert resources away from the root causes of social issues, and sideline important measures of impact for short-term political gain and power.

Today, many evaluations continue to carry the echoes of historical power dynamics. These evaluations, conducted with the ostensible aim of improving social programs and public investments, often unintentionally perpetuate systems of control, subjugation and cultural erasure. It is a paradox – evaluation, designed to promote positive change, inadvertently perpetuates harm.

Alternatively, culturally safe evaluation transcends a one-size-fits-all approach. It should strive to be fit-for-purpose and context-specific; acknowledge the diversity of participants in community-engaged projects; ensure their voices, beliefs and needs are respected throughout the entire process; and remain attuned to the broader community ecosystem that's always existed and forever changing.

The evaluation ensemble

To understand culturally safe evaluation, it's important to have an awareness of the 'evaluation ensemble' – three interconnected and overlapping elements that are found in all types of evaluations, no matter the sector: the evaluand, the evaluation and the evaluator.

- The evaluand (project): this represents the subject or object undergoing evaluation, which in the arts, culture and community sector could encompass a diverse range of projects. Examples include arts programs and events, cultural heritage initiatives, community development projects, cultural exchange and diversity workshops, educational initiatives in the arts and culture, social inclusion and access programs, creative-industries support programs, public art and urban design projects, health and wellbeing initiatives, and environmental and sustainability campaigns.
- The evaluation (process or product): each evaluand requires a tailored evaluation approach and methodology to assess a specific component of the evaluand, reflected in a program logic (see 'The evaluator's toolkit' on the next page). The Better Evaluation website has a fantastic menu of evaluation approaches with useful explanations

on which contexts they are most useful for. Once those are in place, the process (evaluation) is a dynamic and iterative activity that assesses the effectiveness and impact of community-engaged projects. It involves collecting, analysing and using data to understand changes in outcomes and impacts. Evaluations can take different forms, either running parallel to the project or as a product used within the process. Evaluation projects may include comprehensive reports, bite-sized insights, or dashboards with key conclusions and recommendations.

- The evaluator (people): in the arts, culture and community sectors, the evaluator is the individual or team responsible for leading the evaluation activities. Ideally, this responsibility should be given to a person who does not have any conflict of interest, though it is not at all uncommon for the lead artist, cultural leader or community practitioner to take on the role of evaluator.

Understanding the evaluation ensemble and how they influence each other is essential for conducting an evaluation that aligns with the community's needs, aspirations and unique context. When the ensemble works in harmony, the evaluation process is designed in parallel with the needs of the project (the evaluand) and aligned with the cultural strengths and values of a respectful and self-aware evaluator. This increases the likelihood of a successful and culturally safe evaluation.

The evaluator's toolkit

In community-engaged projects, evaluations always involve some degree of collaboration with other stakeholders. This collaborative effort makes the evaluand more complex.

There is one useful tool in an evaluator's toolbox that can help sort these complexities and focus the evaluation on certain components that need to be evaluated. This is called a program logic (also known as a logic model, log frame or theory of change). A program logic is essentially a map or flowchart that illustrates the key steps required for your project to reach its intended outcome or impact. You can create your logic map by thinking about the following components and questions, and piecing them together to tell a complete story:

- Context and situation: why is the project needed? What is the social problem or issue? For whom is it an issue? What are the circumstances of the target group? Are there other existing services or projects that are attempting to address the same issue? Where/why are they not working? How will your project attempt to address some or all of the gaps?
- Goals and objectives: what is our priority? What shared goals will the project focus on to address the issue and gaps?
- Resources: what do you have to invest? What resources will you need to successfully deliver the project?
- Activities: what will you deliver? What activities will the project involve – separately or in collaboration with others? How often will these activities be done

and for how long? Where will they be delivered?

- External factors: what factors (outside of your project's scope and control) could affect the activity?
- Outputs: what will be produced? What do funders or stakeholders require?
  - » Short-term outcomes (during the project): what changes do you expect to see in participants while they are engaged in the activity?
  - » Medium-term outcomes (at or shortly after the end of the project): what changes do you expect to see before participants finish the activity? What changes do you expect to influence within one month?
  - » Long-term outcomes (after the project): what changes do you expect to contribute towards after the project period?

The evaluation framework

Effective evaluation is not just a routine exercise – it demands a thoughtful and systematic approach that considers the unique cultural contexts of the communities involved.

The following steps are based on the Framework for Program Evaluation created by the American Centers for Disease Control and Infection (CDC), which harmonises the specific context of an evaluand with a systematic, six-stage evaluation process that's underpinned by principles of cultural respect and reciprocity.

Stage 1: Engage people with a genuine approach

- Engagement lies at the heart of culturally safe practice and can transform the power dynamics of an evaluation.
- Advocate for authentic relationship building with community members by identifying and involving key stakeholders such as Elders, leaders and representatives in all stages of the evaluation process to foster trust and ensure that the evaluation aligns with community priorities.
- Emphasise the significance of reciprocity by recognising community members as active participants rather than passive subjects, and acknowledging and valuing the community's expertise and contributions. A genuine engagement approach is formalised, resourced and embedded at all stages of the evaluation.

Stage 2: Understand the evaluand

- In the pursuit of culturally safe practice, we need to delve deep into the heart of the program's goals and objectives. Consider using a program logic tool to map out the key components of the evaluand. Use the program logic questions mentioned above to populate each component.
- A nuanced understanding from the community's perspective is imperative to frame evaluation questions that are culturally relevant and resonate with their aspirations. This process involves immersing ourselves in the cultural fabric and histories of the communities we serve.

- Consider cultural relevance in framing evaluation questions to ensure they are meaningful and context-specific.

Stage 3: Tailor the evaluation design

- To recognise the diversity of knowledge systems, use a flexible evaluation design that accommodates different ways of knowing.
- Embrace a mixed-method approach that blends Western evaluation techniques with culturally appropriate data-collection methods to ensure comprehensive and meaningful quantitative and qualitative data that captures the essence of the community.

Stage 4: Ensure respectful data collection and analysis

- Data collection and analysis become transformative and respectful when cultural protocols are meticulously followed and we ensure that the data collected is used for the betterment of the community.
- Gather multiple sources of data to strengthen the evaluation's validity and reliability.
- Obtain informed consent from participants; respect cultural protocols and privacy considerations.
- Use culturally appropriate data-collection tools and methods that resonate with the community.

Stage 5: Create new insights and weave the project impact story

- The pivotal moment when all sources of data are analysed, crafted into key themes and new insights that address the key evaluation questions is called 'sensemaking'. This should be a collaborative process that involves community members who participated in the data collection or are direct beneficiaries of the project being evaluated.
- Use storytelling and culturally sensitive communication methods to craft an evaluation narrative that resonates with the community and acknowledges diverse perspectives.

Stage 6: Use and share learnings

- Evaluation findings must not merely gather dust on a shelf; they should actively inform improvements and community decision-making.
- Work hand-in-hand with community members to co-create learning and action plans based on evaluation findings.
- Empower the community to take ownership of the evaluation findings, creating culturally safe spaces for shared learning and collective reflections as a whole community.
- Share evaluation outcomes with stakeholders in accessible formats, encouraging dialogue and collective learning.

....

Things to keep in mind

Culturally safe evaluation in community-engaged projects goes beyond traditional evaluation methods. By embracing cultural awareness, inclusivity and respect, evaluators can enhance the rigour and relevance of evaluation processes and products. To embark on a culturally safe evaluation journey, meaningful engagement with all stakeholders is essential.

* Planning: at the earliest opportunity (for example, during ideation, planning or pre-implementation), outline the critical parts of the evaluation ensemble and how they interconnect.
* Engagement: engaging and understanding the perspectives of commissioners, funders, project staff and beneficiaries is vital. Co-designing the evaluation process and including all parties in the development of the key evaluation questions ensures diverse perspectives are considered, and co-ownership of the process and outcomes.
* Community ownership and empowerment: culturally safe evaluation practices prioritise community ownership and empowerment. By involving community members in decision-making processes, their experiences and insights are valued, leading to more meaningful evaluation outcomes.
* Relational accountability: working with marginalised communities requires us to identify realistic indicators that we can use to track our engagement efforts over time (such as genuine participation, empowerment and ownership, inclusion, two-way communication, adaptability, localisation or building

on local capacity). Culturally safe evaluation practices emphasise respectful and trusting relationships to foster meaningful knowledge generation.

* Embrace continuous learning and adaptation: evaluation is an iterative process that requires ongoing learning and adaptation. Culturally safe evaluators adopt a growth mindset, embracing feedback and using evaluation findings to improve programs.
* Emphasise ethical considerations: recognising and respecting cultural protocols, confidentiality and privacy are key, as is prioritising the wellbeing and safety of community members throughout the evaluation process.
* Self-reflection: culturally safe evaluation practice requires evaluators to engage in self-reflection and introspection on their beliefs, values, biases and assumptions. Understanding one's cultural background, biases and experiences is essential in ensuring objectivity and inclusivity in engaging with diverse communities.
* Motivations and attitudes: cultivate a mindset of humility, curiosity and openness to learning from the community. Respect, empathy and willingness to listen and understand are key attitudes to establish trust and empower community members.
* Evaluative thinking and decision-making: cultivate critical-thinking skills to analyse and interpret data, and make informed decisions based on evidence.

The relationship is the project

By Jade Lillie

A relationship is the state of being connected. Without connection to the people we are working with, we're not able to design or create a truly community-engaged process or experience.

In community-engaged practice, the most important element of the work is to develop and nurture our relationships: between ourselves, community members, partner organisations, investors, and of course, the creative practitioners/project team. Like any other relationships, these connections need tending to – before, during and after our key project milestones, our celebratory moments and, of course, during our epic fails.

People first

Key to great community-engaged practice is the people involved in making it happen, and the possibilities that exist within the relationships you have with those people.

People make projects possible. It seems simple to say that 'the relationship is the project', but it's often the thing that gets lost among deadlines, egos, lack of experience, shame, bias, time, external expectations and our busy lives.

While there are many other elements that go into creating a successful project, if the relationships are robust, they will generally be able to withstand all kinds of disruptions, changes and failures. A good set of relationships should allow you to collectively address disappointments and surprises, and identify the way forward in any crisis. A level of personal and professional investment, time and communication is required to create the best possible environment for those relationships to grow, flourish, and (when necessary) to end well.

Key relationships in community-engaged practices

- Community. Obviously, the relationship/s you have with any community are essential in any community-engaged context. It's important these relationships are diverse, intersectional, cross-sector and wide-ranging. They may include arts and non-arts relationships. In regional and remote areas, for example, most of your relationships may be with non-arts partners.
- Facilitators (artists/producers). Essentially, a community-engaged arts project is a collaboration between artists and communities. The relationships with artists on the project are vital to its success. Focus on ensuring that the facilitator has the greatest possible opportunity to carry out their role as creative practitioner collaborating with communities.
- Facilitators (others). If you are working with communities in a non-arts context, think about

---

who might be your key collaborators, makers
or facilitators. For example, in a health setting,
this person might work in health promotion or
in a regional council, perhaps a social planner
or economic development officer.

- Stakeholders. These may include investors,
project partners, funding bodies and
organisations. For example, you may partner
with an organisation that is not based in the
community but that can offer an important
service that the community needs.

Who is responsible for your relationships?

Most community-engaged projects will have a lead
facilitator, producer or project manager who will act as
the 'face' of a project and who will, ideally, be responsible
for developing and managing relationships from the
beginning to the end. It is important, however, to make
sure that this role isn't left entirely to one person, and
that other people share those connections in case of
change, departure or succession.

We can also run into trouble if the person who
is leading the project acts as a 'gatekeeper' between
communities, artists and key stakeholders. This is
another reason why having a range of people engaged
in the building and maintenance of relationships is
important.

Know yourself. No matter how hard we may try, we
won't get along with everyone all the time. It's human
nature. But this can have a huge impact on community-

engaged projects. It's OK if you're not the right person for a particular project or community group – step outside of yourself and find the person who is. If you're unsure, have a conversation with a collaborator or colleague about your concerns – ideally, speak with someone who knows your practice and your skills.

Know your skills. If you're not a good relationship builder, if you do not like talking on the phone or in person, or solving problems collectively, then the role of lead facilitator/producer is not going to be for you. Similarly, if you have difficulty articulating a problem or having difficult conversations, the primary facilitation role is not going to be for you either. Hold yourself to account – know your strengths and your weaknesses.

··

Things to keep in mind

Relationships are unpredictable and complex, but there are ways we can work to hold them with respect and transparency.

* First Peoples first. Always start by asking what it means to consider First Peoples first in the context of your work, your project and your relationships. Living and working in Australia is a complex and colonised space. To work in an arts and cultural context is exactly that – Australian culture. Australia's First People are the first artists, storytellers and activists.

* Start the way you want to finish. Ideally, some of the relationships will be in place before the idea is developed. You can then develop the idea with key collaborators from the very beginning. It helps to

ensure that building relationships is simply part of your practice, your citizenship – the way you are (or want to be) in the world.

∗ Make the effort. If you are interested in working with a particular community that is not your own, show up to things that are important to the people you are working with. Make sure you are present at the moments that mean something to the community, to meet people and learn things. This is when the relationship starts to be reciprocal. If you want to be in deeper relationships with First Nations artists and communities, consider whether you have shown your commitment. Have you attended an Invasion Day rally or NAIDOC Week event? Have you undertaken Indigenous-led training in working in First Nations cultural contexts (see the chapter 'First Peoples first')?

∗ Be an ally. When you're connected to a community, you need to actively pay attention to the issues that are important to them, speak up about the inequities that exist and take proactive steps to change them. If you're not willing or ready to support the people you're working with, it may not be the right project for you. As queer disabled performer Kochava Lilit writes, 'Ally means partner, or so I've heard. Someone who cares, who'll be there when the walls fall down. Ally is an action, an alliance you build, not something you identify as'.

∗ Be clear of your motivations. It is essential for you to understand yourself, your biases and privilege. There may be times when you don't fully share the beliefs or values of the people you are working with. It's important to be honest about this and to let the community decide whether to continue working with you or not. Ask yourself what your motivations are for doing the work. If you're not happy to share those motivations (word for word) with the community you are working with, perhaps you're not in it for the right reasons.

* Be respectful. Often, we can 'forget' to include people who may not be obviously engaged in a project but who are important in the community. For example, you may be working with young people in a regional community, and you may think involving their parents and carers in the project is unnecessary. Taking them into consideration is essential – not only because they play a key role in supporting the young people to be involved, they also bring knowledge, information and influence and have the authority to stop young people engaging in the project.

* Be honest. Find ways to engage in critical conversations about the development of a project (including what skills and expertise you bring to it), the scale of the ideas, and what the outcomes might be. For example, if a non-arts project partner suggests that a film festival is the best thing for a community, be clear about what would be required to make that happen, but also that there may be other projects that could have more impact in the long-term. Explore all of the options with the people you are working with.

* Don't be a gatekeeper. There can be a tendency (often seen in white, non-community members) to want to 'protect' a community from people who they perceive to work in an unethical way. Rest assured, the community you are working with wasn't lost

or helpless before you came along, and will be very capable of managing relationships for themselves. All you need to do is check with someone that it is OK for you to pass on their details. If they say 'No', there is the answer. If they say 'Yes', go right ahead and move along.

* Stay in your lane. If we want to truly collaborate with communities, we must acknowledge and dismantle the power dynamics that exist in our practices and organisations. This means knowing when you should step aside to make space for peers, friends and colleagues who have less privilege or access than you. Don't apply for roles in a community that could be held by members of that community. Don't speak on a panel about diversity, access, inclusion or any topic for that matter, if you are another white, non-disabled, cisgendered person on a panel full of the same. Assist the organisers to find the right people so there is a balanced perspective.

* Keep adapting. Keep shifting, but always come back to knowing that the relationship is the project.

....

References

What is community-engaged practice?

Larsen, K. (2019). Best practice arts language, retrieved from Larsen Keys website <www.larsenkeys.com.au/2019/07/10/resource-best-practice-arts-language>, accessed 14 August 2023.

First Peoples first

Common Ground. (2023). Explore, retrieved from Common Ground website <www.commonground.org.au/explore>, accessed 14 August 2023.

Land, C. (2015). *Decolonizing Solidarity: Dilemmas and Directions for Supporters of Indigenous Struggles.* London: Zed Books.

Moreton-Robinson, A. M. (2003), I still call Australia home: Indigenous belonging and place in a white postcolonising society, in Ahmed, S., Castada, C., Fortier, A. and Sheller, M. (eds), *Uprootings/Regroundings: Questions of Home and Migration.* London: Routledge.

Rose, D. B. (2004). *Reports from a Wild Country: Ethics for Decolonisation.* Sydney: UNSW Press.

Smith, L. T. (2012). *Decolonizing Methodologies* (2nd edn). London: Zed Books.

Tuck, E., and Yang, K. W. (2012). Decolonization is not a metaphor, *Decolonization: Indigeneity, Education & Society*, 1(1), 1–40.

Watego, C. (2021). *Another Day in the Colony.* Brisbane: University of Queensland Press.

Wolfe, P. (1999). *Settler Colonialism and the Transformation of Anthropology.* London: Cassell.

Cultural safety

Ahmed, S. (2006). The nonperformativity of antiracism, *Meridians*, 7(1), 104–126.

Ahmed, S. (2012). *On Being Included: Racism and Diversity in Institutional Life.*

Australia Council for the Arts. (2015). Arts nation: An overview of Australian arts, retrieved from Creative Australia website <www.creative.gov.au/advocacy-and-research/arts-nation-an-overview-of-australian-arts>, accessed 1 September 2023.

Australia Council for the Arts. (2020). Towards equity: A research overview of diversity in Australia's arts and cultural sector, retrieved from Creative Australia website <www.creative.gov.au/advocacy-and-research/towards-equity-a-research-overview-of-diversity-in-australias-arts-and-cultural-sector>, accessed 1 September 2023.

Butler, A. (2017). Safe white spaces, retrieved from Runway website <www.runway.org.au/safe-white-spaces>, accessed 14 August 2023.

De Souza, R. (2018). Busting five myths about cultural safety – please take note, Sky News et al., retrieved from Croakey website <www.croakey.org/busting-five-myths-about-cultural-safety-please-take-note-sky-news-et-al>, accessed 14 August 2023.

Land, C. (2015). *Decolonizing Solidarity: Dilemmas and Directions for Supporters of Indigenous Struggles.* London: Zed Books.

Nursing Council of New Zealand. (2011). Guidelines for cultural safety, the Treaty of Waitangi and Maori health in nursing education and practice, retrieved from Nursing Council of New Zealand website <www.nursingcouncil.org.nz/Public/Nursing/Standards_and_guidelines/NCNZ/nursing-section/Standards_and_guidelines_for_nurses.aspx?hkey=9fc06ae7-a853-4d10-b5fe-992cd44ba3de>, accessed 14 August 2023.

Smith, A., Funaki, H., and MacDonald, L. (2021). Living, breathing settler-colonialism: The reification of settler norms in a common university space. *Higher Education Research & Development*, 40(1), 132–145.

Taylor, K., and Guerin, P. (2010). *Health Care and Indigenous Australians: Cultural Safety in Practice.* Melbourne: Macmillan Education.

Throsby, D., and Petetskaya, K. (2017). Making art work: An economic study of professional artists in Australia, retrieved from Creative Australia website <www.creative.gov.au/advocacy-and-research/making-art-work>, accessed 1 September 2023.

Racial literacy: What is 'race' and why is it so important to understand?

Brown, L. (2012). Race matters in context: Silence, empowerment and racial literacy in Australia from the 'other' perspective, Honours thesis, University of Melbourne.

Brown, L., Kelada, O. and Jones, D. (2021). 'While I knew I was raced, I didn't think much of it': The need for racial literacy in decolonising classrooms, *Postcolonial Studies*, 24(1), 82–103, <https://doi.org/10.1080/13688790.2020.1759755>.

Dyer, R. (1997). *White: Essays on Race and Culture*. New York: Routledge.

Guinier, L. (2004). From racial liberalism to racial literacy: Brown v. Board of Education and the interest-divergence dilemma. *Journal of American History* 91(1), 92–118.

Jones, D. (2000). *Shearing the Rams* [painting]. Ink jet print on treated canvas mounted on Kappa board using Gloy 870, Art Gallery of Western Australia. © Dianne Jones / Copyright Agency.

Twine, F. W. (2004). A white side of Black Britain: The concept of racial literacy. *Ethnic and Racial Studies* 27(6), 876–907.

Intersectionality in community

Cooper, B. C., Morris, S. M. and Boylorn, R.M. (eds) (2017). *The Crunk Feminist Collection*. New York: The Feminist Press.

Claire. (2016). Intersectionality – a definition, history, and guide, retrieved from Sister Outrider website <https://sisteroutrider.wordpress.com/2016/07/27/intersectionality-a-definition-history-and-guide>, accessed 14 August 2023.

Community Reading Room (2023). <communityreadingroom.com>, accessed 14 August 2023.

Crenshaw, K. (2016). On Intersectionality keynote, retrieved from Women of the World on YouTube <www.youtube.com/watch?v=-DW4HLgYPlA>, accessed 14 August 2023.

Davis, A. in Jones, D. (2006), Angela Davis: Remaking the world, retrieved from UC Davis website <www.ucdavis.edu/news/angela-davis-remaking-world>, accessed 14 August 2023.

Lilla International Women's Network (2019). <www.lillanetwork.wordpress.com/about>, accessed 14 August 2023.

Lorde, A. (1984 and 2007). Age, race, class and sex: women redefining difference, in Lorde, A., *Sister Outsider: Essays and Speeches*. California: Crossing Press.

Moroccan Soup Bar (2017). Speed date a Muslim, retrieved from ABC website <www.abc.net.au/religion/watch/compass/speed-date-a-muslim/10142432>, accessed 14 August 2023.

Pruit, S. (2017, 2022). The man behind Black History Month, retrieved from History.com website <www.history.com/news/the-man-behind-black-history-month>, accessed 14 August 2023.

Ethics and self-determination

Alcoff, L. (1992). The problem with speaking for others, *Journal of Cultural Critique*, 1(20), 5–32.

Austin, W. J. (2008). Relational ethics, in Given, L. M. (ed.), *The SAGE Encyclopaedia of Qualitative Research Methods*. Thousand Oaks: Sage.

Cañas, T. (2015). 10 things you need to consider if you are an artist, not of the refugee and asylum seeker community, looking to work with our community, <https://aktiontanz.de/wp-content/uploads/2017/03/RISE-statement-on-working-with-the-refugee-community.pdf>.

Cañas, T. (2017). Diversity is a white word, retrieved from ArtsHub website <www.artshub.com.au/education/news-article/opinions-and-analysis/professional-development/tania-canas/diversity-is-a-white-word-252910>, accessed 14 August 2023.

hooks, b. (1994). *Teaching to Transgress: Education as the Practice of Freedom*, New York: Routledge.

Montero, M. (2007). The political psychology of liberation: from politics to ethics and back, *Political Psychology* 28(5), 517–533.

Resnik, D. (2013). What is ethics in research and why is it important, National Institute of Environmental Health Sciences, retrieved from Verona Schools website <www.veronaschools.org/cms/lib02/NJ01001379/Centricity/Domain/588/What%20is%20Ethics%20in%20Research%20Why%20is%20it%20Important.pdf>, accessed 14 August 2023.

Sonn, C. and Baker, A. (2016). Creating inclusive knowledges: exploring the transformative potential of arts and cultural practice, *International Journal of Inclusive Education*, 20(3), 215–228.

Thiong'o, N. (1986). *Decolonising the Mind: The Politics of Language in African Literature*, Nairobi: East African Publishers.

The art of facilitation

Sheedy, B. (2021). Communication and learning styles, in Larsen, K. (2021), Our Hybrid Future, retrieved from Our Hybrid Future website <www.ourhybridfuture.com.au>, accessed 14 August 2023.

Disability access and inclusion

Heumann, J. (1982). Speaking, in Lacy, S. and London, J. (2018), *Freeze Frame: Room for Living Room*, San Francisco, retrieved from Suzanne Lacy on Vimeo <www.vimeo.com/263690756>, accessed 14 August 2023.

Koch, J. (2010). Find your own pace and move together: the application of universal design of instruction in dance degrees in higher education, retrieved from Jürg Koch website <static1.squarespace.com/static/537f912ce4b0f33d47e8549a/t/5880a049be6594efd28522d0/1484824650400/Koch+UD+in+Dance+web+17.pdf>, accessed 22 August 2023.

RL Mace Universal Design Institute. (2023). What is universal design?, retrieved from RL Mace Universal Design Institute website <www.udinstitute.org/what-is-ud>, accessed 14 August 2023.

United Nations, International Day of Persons with Disabilities, 3 December, retrieved from United Nations website <www.un.org/en/observances/day-of-persons-with-disabilities/background>, accessed 22 August 2023.

Bridging Deaf and hearing worlds

Bone, T. A., Wilkinson, E., Ferndale, D., and Adams, R. (2022). Indigenous and Deaf people and the implications of ongoing practices of colonization: A comparison of Australia and Canada. *Humanity & Society*, 46(3), 495–521, <https://doi.org/10.1177/01605976211001575>.

Branson, J., and Miller, D. (1993). Sign language, the deaf and the epistemic violence of mainstreaming. *Language and Education*, 7(1), 21–41, <https://doi.org/10.1080/09500789309541346>.

Ladd, P. (2003). *Understanding Deaf Culture: In Search of Deafhood*. Bristol: Multilingual Matters.

Martin, S. (2023), interview with Claire Bridge and Chelle Destefano.

Wright, D. (2023), interview with Claire Bridge and Chelle Destefano.

Labels: From avoidance to acceptance

Ralph, N. (2018). Understanding disability: Part 6 – the radical model, retrieved from Drake Music website <www.drakemusic.org/blog/nim-ralph/understanding-disability-part-6-the-radical-model>, accessed 14 August 2023.

Withers, A.J. (2012). Radical model, retrieved from Still My Revolution website <www.stillmyrevolution.org/2012/01/01/radical-model>, accessed 14 August 2023.

Creative lives and contemporary ageing

Rungie, M. (2023). The ingredients to 'ageing well', retrieved from ABC Radio National website <www.abc.net.au/radionational/programs/bigideas/the-ingredients-to-ageing-well-/14138922>, accessed 14 August 2023.

Village Landais, The establishment, retrieved from Village Landais website <villagealzheimer.landes.fr/en/the-establishment>, accessed 14 August 2023.

World Health Organization. (2022). Ageing and health, retrieved from World Health Organization website <www.who.int/news-room/fact-sheets/detail/ageing-and-health>, accessed 14 August 2023.

Working with queer communities and artists

Alinsky, S. D. (1971). *Rules for Radicals*, New York: Random House.

Aranjuez, A. (2017). The abstraction of privilege, retrieved from Right Now website <www.rightnow.org.au/creative-works/the-abstraction-of-privilege>, accessed 16 August 2023.

Centers for Disease Control and Infection (CDC) Office of Readiness and Response and Substance Abuse and Mental Health Services Administration's National Center for Trauma-Informed Care (2014). 6 guiding principles to a trauma-informed approach, retrieved from CDC website <www.cdc.gov/orr/infographics/6_principles_trauma_info.htm>, accessed 14 August 2023.

Law, B. (2012). *Gaysia*, Melbourne: Black Inc.

RuPaul's *Drag Race* (2009–2023). World of Wonder.

Ryan, C., and Jetha, C. (2010). *Sex at Dawn: The Prehistoric Origins of Modern Sexuality*, Melbourne: Scribe.

Queer Eye (2018–2023). Scout Productions for Netflix.

Wallman, S. (2016). A covert gaze at conservative gays, retrieved from The Nib website <www.thenib.com/a-covert-gaze-at-conservative-gays>, accessed 14 August 2023.

Gender and public spaces

Castricum, C. with Transgender Victoria and Queerspace (2021). Gender diversity guidelines, best practice guidelines for live music venues, retrieved from Music Victoria website <www.musicvictoria.com.au/resources/best-practice-guidelines-for-live-music-venues>, accessed 14 August 2023.

Costanza-Chock, S. (2020). *Design Justice: Community-Led Practices to Build the Worlds We Need*, Cambridge: MIT Press.

Messih, S., and Barry, A. (2019). Clear expectations: Guidelines for institutions, galleries and curators working with trans, non-binary and gender diverse artists in Australia, retrieved from NAVA website <www.visualarts.net.au/guides/2019/clear-expectations>, accessed 14 August 2023.

No-one here talks about class
Australia Council for the Arts. (2020). Towards Equity: A research overview of diversity in Australia's arts and cultural sector, retrieved from Creative Australia website <www.creative.gov.au/advocacy-and-research/towards-equity-a-research-overview-of-diversity-in-australias-arts-and-cultural-sector>, accessed 1 September 2023.
Sheppard, J., and Biddle, N. (2015). ANU Poll 19: Social class in Australia beyond the 'working and 'middle' classes, Canberra: Australian Data Archive, retrieved from ANU website <www.csrm.cass.anu.edu.au/sites/default/files/docs/ANUPoll-social-class-sept-2015_0.pdf>, accessed 15 August 2023.

Platforming for community: Going beyond surface representation
Aranjuez, A. (2019). Beyond shared trauma: the identity crisis – forging a path forward. *Australian Rationalist*, 115, 22–27.
Benhabib, S. (1992). Utopian dimension in communicative ethics, in Ingram, D., and Simon-Ingram, J. (eds) (1992). *Critical Theory: The Essential Readings*. New York: Paragon House.
Bourdieu, P. (1986). The forms of capital, in Richardson, J. (ed.) (1986). *Handbook of Theory and Research for the Sociology of Education*, Westport: Greenwood.
Charlton, J. I. (1998). *Nothing About Us Without Us: Disability Oppression and Empowerment*. Berkeley: University of California Press.
Collins, P. H. (2000). *Black Feminist Thought: Knowledge, Consciousness, and the Politics of Empowerment*. New York: Routledge.
Crenshaw, K. (1991). Mapping the margins: Intersectionality, identity politics, and violence against women of color. *Stanford Law Review*, 43(6), 1241–1299.
Fraser, N. (2000). Rethinking recognition, *New Left Review*, 3, 107–118.

Jackson, C. (2013). The legacy of Lt. Uhura: Astronaut Mae Jemison on race in space, retrieved from Duke Today website <www.today.duke.edu/2013/10/maejemison>, accessed
14 August 2023.

Leong, N. (2021). *Identity Capitalism: The Powerful Insiders Who Exploit Diversity to Maintain Inequality.* Stanford: Stanford University Press.

Phillips, A. (2004). Defending equality of outcome. *Journal of Political Philosophy,* 12(1), 1–19.

Stewart, D. (2017). Language of appeasement, retrieved from Inside Higher Ed website <www.insidehighered.com/views/2017/03/30/colleges-need-language-shift-not-one-you-think-essay>, accessed 14 August 2023.

Young, I. M. (1997). Asymmetrical reciprocity: on moral respect, wonder, and enlarged thought. *Constellations,* 3(3), 340–363.

Audiences and cultural diversity

Australian Bureau of Statistics. (2022), 2021 Census: Nearly half of Australians have a parent born overseas, retrieved from ABS website <www.abs.gov.au/media-centre/media-releases/2021-census-nearly-half-australians-have-parent-born-overseas>, accessed 14 August 2023.

.id. (2021). Australia: Language used at home, retrieved from .idcommunity website <www.profile.id.com.au/australia/language>, accessed 14 August 2023.

Kapetopoulos, F. (2009). Adjust your view: Developing multicultural audiences for the arts, a toolkit, retrieved from Australia Council website <www.australiacouncil.gov.au/__data/assets/pdf_file/0017/73511/Adjust_Your_View_Toolkit_4April2010.pdf>, accessed 4 April 2010.

Megalogenis, G. (2019). Australasia rising: Who we are becoming?, retrieved from the *Sydney Morning Herald* website <www.smh.com.au/national/australasia-rising-who-we-are-becoming-20190122-p50ssx.html>, accessed 16 August 2023.

UNESCO. (2003). Intangible cultural heritage, text of the convention for the safeguarding of the intangible cultural heritage, retrieved from UNESCO website <ich.unesco.org/en/convention>, accessed 14 August 2023.

Walker Kuhne, D. (2005). Invitation to the Party: Building Bridges to the Arts, Culture and Community. New York: Theater Communications Group.

Walker Kuhne, D. (2003 and 2007). Invitation to the Party public lectures. Melbourne: Kape Communications Pty Ltd.

Art and climate justice

350.org Australia. (2023). Cut all ties, retrieved from Cut All Ties website <cutallties.350.org.au>, accessed 14 August 2023.

Burke, K. (2021). Perth's Fringe World festival parts way with mining giant Woodside, retrieved from *The Guardian* website <www.theguardian.com/culture/2021/jun/04/perths-fringe-world-festival-parts-way-with-mining-giant-woodside>, accessed 14 August 2023.

City of Melbourne through Arts House in partnership with the Research Unit of Public Cultures, Melbourne University (2021). In the time of refuse collection, retrieved from Arts House website <www.artshouse.com.au/events/in-the-time-of-refuge-collection>, accessed 14 August 2023.

De Vietri, G. (2019). Fossil fuels + the Arts, Maps of Gratitude Lumps of Coal and Cones of Silence, retrieved from Gabrielle de Vietri on Vimeo <www.vimeo.com/337663497>, accessed 14 August 2023.

De Vietri, G. (2019). Maps of Gratitude, retrieved from Gabrielle De Vietri website <www.gabrielledevietri.net/maps-of-gratitude>, accessed 14 August 2023.

Disability and Philanthropy Forum (2023). Connections between climate change and disability, retrieved from Disability and Philanthropy Forum website <www.disabilityphilanthropy.org/resource/connections-between-climate-change-and-disability/?fbclid=IwAR2wADtxQILZw1GMLyagIZpYHu2nvMPw6ob8rbdmeoxDJRSoc7quAjfC6Nw>, accessed 15 August 2023.

Evans, M. (2015). *Artwash: Big Oil and the Arts*. London: Pluto Press.

Evans, M. (2015). Take the Money and Run, Artwash: Big Oil and the Arts new book intro by Mel Evans, for 'Take

the Money and Run?' event, retrieved from YouTube
<www.youtube.com/watch?v=12mm7Srj1WU>, accessed
14 August 2023.

Ghosh, A. (2016). *The Great Derangement: Climate Change
and the Unthinkable*. Chicago: University of Chicago Press.

Global Witness (2021). What is Climate Justice?, retrieved
from Global Witness website <www.globalwitness.org/en/
blog/what-climate-justice>, accessed 14 August 2023.

Groundwater Arts. (2023). Divest to Invest, retrieved from
Groundwater Arts website <www.groundwaterarts.com/
divest-to-invest.html>, accessed 14 August 2023.

International Climate Justice Network (2002). Bali Principles
of Climate Justice, retrieved from Corp Watch website
<www.corpwatch.org/article/bali-principles-climate-
justice>, accessed 14 August 2023.

Kelly, A., and Ludlum, S. (2022), Climate Crisis and the Arts:
Untangling: Breaking up with Fossil Fuels, Adelaide Writers
Week, retrieved from YouTube <www.youtube.com/
watch?v=CTzHcVpnipk>, accessed 14 August 2023.

Klein, N. (2014). *This Changes Everything: Capitalism
Versus the Climate*. New York: Simon and Schuster.

Liberate Tate (2016). Liberate Tate with the Guerrilla
Girls call on Tate: Go 'fossil funds free', retrieved from
Liberate Tate website <www.liberatetate.wordpress.
com/2016/10/06/liberate-tate-with-the-guerrillagirls-
tate-go-fossilfundsfree>, accessed 14 August 2023.

Morgan, T., and Mitchell, A. (2022). Darwin Festival won't
accept $200k in funding from group of philanthropists
to replace Santos sponsorship, retrieved from ABC
News website <www.abc.net.au/news/2022-12-15/nt-
darwin-festival-funding-falls-through-fossil-free-arts-
nt/101775768>, accessed 14 August 2023.

National Association of Visual Arts (NAVA) (2022). Code of
practice: Climate adaptation and environmental action,
retrieved from NAVA website <code.visualarts.net.au/
principles-ethics-and-rights/climate-adaptability-and-
justice/recommended-resources>, accessed 14 August 2023.

Nolan, K. (2020). First Nations resistance and Climate Justice,
The Commons Social Change Library, retrieved from
Commons Library website <www.commonslibrary.org/

reset-1-first-nations-resistance-climate-justice>, accessed
14 August 2023.
Original Power. (2023). Self determination, retrieved from
Original Power website <www.originalpower.org.au/self_
determination>, accessed 5 September 2023.
Sherry, E., Karg, A., Golding, D., and Bramley, O. (2023).
*Bad Romance: Coal, Gas and Oil Sponsorship in the
Australia Arts Industry.* Melbourne: 350 Australia.
Sierra Club. (2023). History of Environmental Justice,
retrieved from Sierra Club website <www.sierraclub.org/
environmental-justice/history-environmental-justice>,
accessed 14 August 2023.

Creative practice in disaster recovery

Creative Recovery Network (2023). Creative Recovery
Handbook.
Social Recovery Reference Group Australia (2018). National
Principles for Disaster Recovery, retrieved from Australian
Disaster Resilience Knowledge Hub website <www.
knowledge.aidr.org.au/resources/national-principles-for-
disaster-recovery>, accessed 14 August 2023.

Reworlding: Adapting to the climate emergency through relationality

Barlo, S., Boyd, W. E., Hughes, M., Wilson, S., and Pelizzon, A.
(2021). Yarning as protected space: relational accountability
in research. *AlterNative: An International Journal of
Indigenous Peoples,* 17(1), 40–48.
Campbell, M., in Lee, E. V. (2016), Reconciling in the
Apocalypse, The Monitor, retrieved from Policy Alternatives
website <www.policyalternatives.ca/publications/monitor/
reconciling-apocalypse>, accessed 14 August 2023.
Rae, J. (2019–2021), Portage, Arts House, Melbourne,
retrieved from Jen Rae website <www.jenraeis.com/
portage-raft-flotilla-shelter2camp>, accessed
4 September 2023.
Rae, J., and Coleman, C. G. (2021). First Assembly
of the Centre for Reworlding, Arts House, Melbourne
retrieved from Jen Rae website <www.jenraeis.com/

first-assembly-of-the-centre-for-reworlding-1>, accessed
4 September 2023.

Rae, J., and Coleman, C. G. (2023). Reworlding: Speculative
futuring in the endtimes in the everywhen, in Hjorth, L.,
Jungknickel, K., Lammes, S., and Rae, J. (eds), Failurists:
When things go awry, *Theory on Demand* #47, 69–78.

Stanner, T. E. H. (2009). The Dreaming [1953], in
The Dreaming and Other Essays. Melbourne: Black Inc.

Wilson, S. (2008). *Research Is Ceremony: Indigenous
Research Methods*. Black Point: Fernwood Publishing.

Squads and swarms: Engaging with communities online

Australian Digital Inclusion Index (2023), retrieved
from Australian Digital Inclusion Index website
<digitalinclusionindex.org.au>, accessed 14 August 2023.

Jurgensen, N. (2011). Digital dualism versus augmented
reality, retrieved from The Society Pages website
<www.thesocietypages.org/cyborgology/2011/02/24/
digital-dualism-versus-augmented-reality>, accessed
14 August 2023.

A duty of care

Australia Council for the Arts. (2023). Protocols and resources,
retrieved from Creative Australia website <www.creative.
gov.au/investment-and-development/protocols-and-
resources>, accessed 1 September 2023.

Culturally safe evaluation

Better Evaluation (2023). Evaluation methods and
approaches, retrieved from Better Evaluation website
<www.betterevaluation.org/methods-approaches>,
accessed 5 September 2023.

Centers for Disease Control and Infection (1999).
Framework for program evaluation in public health,
MMWR 1999; 48 (No. RR-11), retrieved from CDC website
<www.cdc.gov/mmwr/PDF/rr/rr4811.pdf>, accessed
15 August 2023.

Royal Children's Hospital Melbourne (2021). Cultural safety
self-evaluation tool, retrieved from Royal Children's

Hospital Melbourne website <www.rch.org.au/
uploadedFiles/Main/Pages/diversity-equity-and-inclusion/
Cultural%20Safety%20-%20Self%20Assessment%20
Tool%20(2021).pdf>, accessed 5 September 2023.
Williams, L. G. (2014). A beneficiary feedback approach
to evaluation: Checklist for evaluators, retrieved
from Beneficiary Feedback in Evaluation website
<www.beneficiaryfeedbackinevaluationandresearch.files.
wordpress.com/2015/03/checklist-for-evaluators.pdf>,
accessed 5 September 2023.

The relationship is the project
Lilit, K. (2017). An open letter to allies, retrieved from
Writers Victoria website <www.writersvictoria.org.au/
writing-life/featured-writers/open-letter-allies>,
accessed 14 August 2023.

Contributors

Esther Anatolitis

Esther Anatolitis is one of Australia's most influential advocates for arts and culture. Esther is Editor of *Meanjin*, Honorary Associate Professor at RMIT School of Art, and a member of the National Gallery of Australia Governing Council. Her strategic consultancy Test Pattern advises institutions and governments on strategy, policy and public space development. A prolific writer and commentator, Esther's work is collected at <estheranatolitis.net>.

Adolfo Aranjuez

Adolfo Aranjuez is an editor, writer, speaker and dancer. He has worked across the publishing and creative arts sectors for 15 years, including editorial tenures for anti-racist literary platform *Liminal*, Australia's oldest screen periodical *Metro*, LGBTQIA+ magazine *Archer* and the Melbourne International Film Festival, as well as collaborations with various cultural, community, educational and government organisations. His essays, criticism and poetry have been published widely in Australia and abroad. <adolfoaranjuez.com>.

Paschal Berry

Paschal Berry is a performance maker, curator, writer and dramaturg whose practice is focused on interdisciplinary, cross-cultural, collaborative and socially engaged processes. He is a creator of award-winning performance works, is an artist mentor, and has contributed works for The Australian Choreographic Centre, Canberra Youth Theatre, QL2,

Performance Space, Urban Theatre Project, Radio National, Belvoir Street Theatre and Blacktown Arts, among others. He has led the programs and education teams of Blacktown Arts, the Biennale of Sydney and the Art Gallery of New South Wales.

Lenine Bourke

Dr Lenine Bourke is an artist, public pedagogue, researcher and consultant who works with people in all kinds of places using all art and cultural forms. She has been the Executive Director of Young People and the Arts Australia, Artistic Director of Contact Inc. and Director of Community Partnerships at Australia Council for the Arts. Her award-winning PhD thesis explored artist-led public pedagogies and created a series of new conceptual works around the climate crisis.

Caroline Bowditch

Caroline Bowditch is currently the CEO at Arts Access Victoria (AAV). She is best known as a performer, maker, teacher, speaker and mosquito buzzing in the ears of the arts industry. Caroline is a regular consultant on access and inclusion internationally, and has also led international residencies in Sweden, Italy, Switzerland and Germany. She is regularly invited to mentor local, national, and international artists at all levels of their artistic development and is on the Board of Creative Australia.

Claire Bridge

Claire Bridge is an artist working across sculpture, painting and moving image, exploring ecological and cultural hybridity. Of Anglo-Indian-Australian and Deaf heritage, Bridge is a hearing grandchild of Deaf Adults, and a former Auslan interpreter and researcher at the National Institute for Deaf Studies. Her major

exhibitions include 'Melbourne Now 2023' at NGV Australia
and 'What I Wish I'd Told You', a touring exhibition of Deaf
Auslan stories, in collaboration with Chelle Destefano and the
Deaf community. <clairebridgeartist.com>.

Jax Brown

Jax Brown (they/them) is an esteemed disability and
LGBTIQA+ rights activist, writer, educator and consultant.
Their tireless commitment to LGBTIQA+ disability human
rights and advocacy has been recognised with a Medal of the
Order of Australia (OAM). Jax utilises their experience as a
queer, trans wheelchair user to explore intersectional identities.
They view disability as a socio-political issue of intersectional
equality, access and human rights and are interested in how
we can build a just and equitable society together.

Lilly Brown

Dr Lilly Brown has spent over a decade supporting
organisations across sectors to develop practices of cultural
safety and racial literacy, and to establish practices that centre
the critical knowledge and lived experience First Nations
people bring to the table. She has a PhD in education from
the University of Melbourne and a masters in politics and
education from the University of Cambridge. Lilly is a
proud Gumbaynggirr woman.

Tania Cañas

Dr Tania Cañas is an artist-researcher based on unceded
Kulin Territory. Tania's work looks at socially engaged and
community-led creative practices as sites of collaboration,
modalities of resistance, as well as ways to rethink processes
and recast institutions. Tania is the Artistic Director at Arts
Gen, a community arts and health organisation.

Simona Castricum

Simona Castricum (she/her) is a multi-disciplinary creative and academic working in music and architecture on Wurundjeri land of Kulin Nation. Simona is a solo musician and producer. In architecture, she is a Postdoctoral Research Fellow at the Melbourne School of Design, University of Melbourne, and an Associate at Parlour: Gender, Equity, Architecture. Simona's speculative and activist creative practice embarks upon queer and trans autofiction and autoethnography.

Seb Chan

Seb Chan is Director and CEO at ACMI in Melbourne. He is also the National President of the Australian Museums and Galleries Association. Seb leads a parallel life in digital art, writing, running music festivals and clubs, and founded Cyclic Defrost Magazine.

Claire G. Coleman

Claire G. Coleman (she/her) is a Noongar author based in Naarm/Melbourne, Victoria. Her debut novel, *Terra Nullius*, won a Norma K. Hemming Award and was shortlisted for the Stella Prize. *Lies, Damn Lies* won the University of Queensland prize for non-fiction, and *Enclave* was longlisted for the Miles Franklin Award. Claire is Co-founder and Writer at the Centre for Reworlding. <www.clairegcoleman.com>.

Ruth De Souza

Dr Ruth De Souza FACN is a nurse, writer, community-engaged researcher, creative practitioner, consultant and host of the Birthing and Justice podcast, featuring conversations about birth, racism and cultural safety to break down the structures built on colonisation. Ruth is a Fellow of The Australian College of Nursing and Honorary Adjunct Professor in the Faculty of

Health and Environmental Sciences – Te Ara Hauora A Pūtaiao at Auckland University of Technology.

Rosie Dennis

Rosie Dennis is the current Artistic Director and CEO of Placemakers* Gold Coast, one of south-east Queensland's leading contemporary arts organisations and producer of the annual BLEACH* and BIG CITY LIGHTS festivals. Rosie was previously Artistic Director and CEO of Urban Theatre Projects, where she curated the award-winning BANKSTOWN:LIVE, conceived and directed the theatrical *Home Country* triptych, and directed two documentaries, *Bre & Back* (SBS) and *One Day for Peace* (ABC).

Chelle Destefano

Chelle Destefano is a Deaf multi-disciplinary artist. She works with textiles, performance, installation, sculpture, painting and drawing to explore culture and identity of her Deaf culture. She is currently focused on dance performance using gestural movements with her Auslan language to speak about her Deaf experiences. Chelle's recent highlights include collaborating with Claire Bridge on a major touring Deaf storytelling project, 'What I Wish I'd Told You', and a major solo performance and exhibition.

Alia Gabres

Alia Gabres is a strategic programming and engagement expert with a speciality in cultural brokerage. She has worked with communities globally for over ten years. She has led strategic programming design and implementation initiatives in various organisations, including non-profits, local governments and start-ups. As a first-generation migrant, she now calls Oakland home by way of Melbourne and Keren, Eritrea. Her favourite title is being called Mama by her baby girl.

Genevieve Grieves

A proud Worimi woman, Genevieve Grieves has more than
20 years experience creating dynamic content for exhibitions,
online, film, television and multimedia. She was the Lead
Curator on the internationally-award winning First Peoples,
a permanent exhibition at Melbourne Museum, and has
developed a range of projects with community engagement
at their heart, including the one-hour documentary for SBS
Television, *Lani's Story* (2013), as well as a place-based
augmented reality experience celebrating Sydney Aboriginal
women, *Barangaroo Ngangamay* (2016).

Alysha Herrmann

Alysha Herrmann (she/her) lives, loves and creates from
regional South Australia. She is an independent creative
producer, writer, performance maker and community
organiser, and is the co-founder of Part of Things. Alysha is
best known for her work collaborating with young people and
regional communities and she is a Regional Arts Australia
Fellow and an Australian Rural Leadership Program Fellow.
She currently serves on the boards of Outback Theatre for
Young People and Carclew. <alyshaherrmann.com>.

Eleanor Jackson

Eleanor Jackson is a Filipino-Australian poet, performer, arts
producer and advocate. She is also Chair of Peril Magazine,
which is dedicated to Asian Australian arts and culture, and
producer of the Melbourne Poetry Map. She is a former Vice-
Chair of The Stella Prize and Board Member of the Queensland
Poetry Festival.

Dianne Jones

Dianne Jones is a visual artist with an interest in historical truths and untruths. She is from Balladong with a particular interest in Aboriginal perspectives within the arts and resistance to popular nationhood ideologies. Dianne guest lectures on Aboriginal Art at the University of Melbourne and has completed her masters at the Victorian College of the Arts. She has exhibited extensively and is in numerous national and international collections.

Samuel Kanaan-Oringo

Samuel Kanaan-Oringo is an artist and support worker who seeks to create mediums and experiences that explore the intersection of the human experience and the nature of reality. Samuel collaborated with Rosie Dennis and Urban Theatre Projects on The Nightline, which featured in UTP's 2018 festival Right Here Right Now. Since then, he has continued to work with UTP as an artist in a young artist collective.

Fotis Kapetopoulos

Fotis Kapetopoulos heads Kape Communications and is English language journalist for Neos Kosmos, Australia's leading Greek Australian masthead He has experience in multicultural services, arts programming, management, audience research, policy development and marketing. Between 1993 and 2001, Fotis was the director for Multicultural Arts Victoria. He holds a BA (Hon.) in politics, a master's in cultural and tourism marketing, an internship from the Smithsonian Institution, Washington, DC and he is a PhD candidate researching multicultural media.

Odette Kelada

Dr Odette Kelada is a lecturer in the School of Culture and Communication at the University of Melbourne. Odette researches and publishes on race, whiteness and gender in Australian writing and the arts. She is interested in the constructions of nation, body and identity in creative representations and the teaching of racial literacy. Her writing has appeared in the *Australian Cultural History Journal*, *Artlink* and the *Australian Critical Race and Whiteness Studies Association Journal*.

Alex Kelly

Alex Kelly (she/her) is an artist, filmmaker and organiser based on Dja Dja Wurrung Country. Alex purposefully connects the disciplines of art and social change. Impact producer on the films *In My Blood It Runs* and Avi Lewis and Naomi Klein's *This Changes Everything*, Alex also has a speculative futures practice, The Things We Did Next and is a member of the Unquiet Collective. <www.echotango.org> | @alexkelly.bsky. social | Instagram @_echotango_.

Cara Kirkwood

Cara Kirkwood (she/her) is a national advocate and influencer for Aboriginal and Torres Strait Islander people, art, culture and creative industries. Currently the Head of Indigenous Engagement and Strategy with the National Gallery of Australia, Cara has previously worked with the Department of Parliamentary Services, Creative Australia, AGSA's Tarnanthi Festival and Desart in Mparntwe (Alice Springs).

Kate Larsen

Kate Larsen (she/her) is a writer, arts and cultural consultant
with more than 25 years experience in the non-profit,
government and cultural sectors in Australia, Asia and the
United Kingdom. Kate is a thought leader in the areas of arts
governance and cultural leadership, workplace culture and
wellbeing, online communication and communities, and
inclusion and community leadership of underrepresented
groups. @KateLarsenKeys.

Jade Lillie

Jade Lillie is a facilitator, consultant and specialist in
community and stakeholder engagement. She has worked
throughout Australia and South-East Asia and is known for
her work in strategy, advocacy, program design, community-
engaged practice and industry development. Jade conceived
The Relationship is the Project following her role as Director
and CEO at Footscray Community Arts (2012–2017) and
curated the first edition as a Sidney Myer Creative Fellow
(2018–2019). <jadelillie.com>.

Tristan Meecham

Tristan Meecham (he/him) is a queer performer and
artist. Together with Bec Reid, he is Artistic Director
of All The Queens Men, an independent arts company
creating contemporary performance in collaboration with
communities. Tristan has become a leading creative voice
within the LGBTIQ+ community nationally and internationally,
specifically for championing the rights of LGBTIQ+ older
people through projects such as the multi award-winning
The Coming Back Out Ball, LGBTIQ+ Elders Dance Club
and Digital Dance Club. <allthequeensmen.net>.

Scotia Monkivitch

Scotia Monkivitch is Executive Officer of the Creative Recovery Network, the national lead agency dedicated to developing and embedding the vital role of culture, creativity and the arts in Australia's disaster management system. She has diverse experience in training, mentoring, strategic planning, project management and research covering all levels of formal education and community engagement. <creativerecovery.net.au>.

Karrina Nolan

Karrina Nolan is a descendant of the Yorta Yorta people, and an experienced manager and organiser of complex programs in Aboriginal communities. She has worked as a facilitator, trainer, researcher and strategist alongside First Nations communities for over 25 years. She dedicated an Atlantic Fellowship to determining how to best build clean-energy projects by and for First Nations people.

Timoci O'Connor

Timoci O'Connor is an I-Kiribati-Fijian-Kiwi with 18 years experience as an evaluation specialist in the public health, education and the arts, cultural and community sectors. He dedicates his time to facilitating evaluative thinking and learning with emerging Indigenous evaluators, and working with community organisations to embed evaluation systems and processes in their work and practice. He also teaches in the Masters of Evaluation and Masters of Public Health at the University of Melbourne.

Lia Pa'apa'a

Lia Pa'apa'a is an artist, creative producer and mama who has cultural connections to Samoa and the Luiseño nation in Southern California. Based in Gimuy (Cairns), Lia works across regional and remote northern Australia. Lia's practice is interdisciplinary and explores the revitalisation, reclamation and reimaging of ancestral practices to support parents, families and communities.

Anthony Peluso

Anthony Peluso (he/him) is Chief Executive/Executive Director at Country Arts SA. He has overseen the organisation's most ambitious changes, working with the many artists and communities, government funders, and corporate and individual supporters who invested time, energy and resources into the organisation's arts programs. Working in regional contexts has broadened his outlook and understanding of his place in the community.

CQ Quinan

CQ Quinan (they/them) is a Senior Lecturer in Gender Studies (School of Culture and Communication) at the University of Melbourne. Their research expertise lies in trans studies and queer theory. CQ is also a key investigator on an EU-based research project that brings together academics, practitioners, NGOs, policymakers and other stakeholders to assess lived experiences of non-binary legal gender recognition.

Jen Rae

Dr Jen Rae (she/they) is an artist-researcher of Canadian Scottish-Métis descent based in Djaara Country/Castlemaine, Victoria. Jen's practice-led expertise is situated at the intersections of art, speculative futures and climate emergency disaster adaptation and resilience. Her work is predominantly articulated through transdisciplinary collaborative methodologies and multi-platform projects, community alliances and public pedagogies. Jen is Co-founder and Creative Research Lead at the Centre for Reworlding and a 2023 Creative Australia Fellow for Emerging and Experimental Art. <www.jenraeis.com, www.centreforreworlding.com>.

Anna Reece

Anna Reece is Artistic Director of Perth Festival. A creative producer, programmer and CEO, she has 20 years of experience, predominantly developed within the context of major multi-arts festivals. Previous roles include Director of Fremantle Arts Centre, where she led the creation of an ambitious new strategic and artistic direction, and Co-CEO of Darwin Festival, where she was instrumental in developing the Lighthouse venue and Festival Park, which transforms the city centre each dry season.

Bec Reid

Bec Reid (she/her) is an Australia-based performer, producer, director and choreographer. A WAAPA graduate, Bec began her professional career as Artistic Director of Stompin in Lutruwita (Tasmania), together with Luke George. Together with art wife Tristan Meecham, Bec is the co-Founder of All The Queens Men and, with Ian Pidd and Kate McDonald, co-created Everybody NOW! Bec's true loves are ceilidhs, Italo Disco and Staffordshire Bull Terriers.

Nina Ross

Nina Ross's practice draws on individual experiences to interrogate the use of political and personal language using video, photography and painting. She works collaboratively, including co-founding Artists' Committee, Artists' Subcommittee, Artists/Parents and Imagining a Future Collective (later Artists' Union). In 2013, Nina received a Master of Fine Art (Research) from Monash University, and was awarded the Vice-Chancellor's Commendation for Master's Excellence Award. <ninaross.com.au>.

Lizzy Sampson

Lizzy Sampson has been making, producing and collaborating in the arts for over a decade. Her contemporary arts practice includes sculpture, painting, installation, photography and text-based works. Lizzy works at both the Australian Research Centre in Sex, Health and Society at La Trobe University and for the Brunswick Women's Choir. She has a Masters of Fine Art, Bachelor of Media Arts and Diploma of Visual Arts. <lizzysampson.com.au>.

Daniel Santangeli

Daniel Santangeli is Artistic Director and Co-CEO of Footscray Community Arts. From 2019 to 2022, Daniel was Chair for Outer Urban Projects, and a board member since 2015. Prior to his time at Footscray Community Arts, Daniel was Program Manager at Midsumma Festival (2016–2019), and previously a producer at Next Wave (2012–2016).

Jessie Scott

Jessie Scott is an independent video artist, writer and programmer working in Narrm (Melbourne) on the stolen lands of the Wurundjeri people of the Kulin nation. She is a founding member of audiovisual art collective Tape Projects, and co-directed and founded the inaugural Channels Video Art Festival in 2013. She is currently completing a PhD in art at RMIT University and raising two children. <jessiescott.tv>.

Jeremy Smith

Jeremy Smith (he/him) lives and plays in Boorloo (Perth). His most recent work includes with Performing Lines as Senior Producer – WA, PICA's General Manager, and the Director of Experimental Arts and Community Arts with Australia Council for the Arts. A core theme of his career has been working closely with artists, organisations and communities to promote artistic bravery, self-determination and authentic representation, and to broker opportunities. Instagram @Jezzalou_77 | X @Jeremy_L_Smith

Thanks

We are grateful for the generosity, thoughtfulness and wisdom of Genevieve, Ruth, Lia, Dianne, Odette, Lilly, Alia, Tania, Eleanor, Samuel, Rosie, Caroline, Claire B, Chelle, Jeremy, Tristan, Bec, Lenine, Daniel, Simona, CQ, Alysha, Anthony, Nina, Lizzy, Jessie, Esther, Anna, Adolfo, Fotis, Karrina, Alex, Scotia, Jen, Claire C, Seb, Paschal and Timoci and for their work in making this extraordinary resource. Thanks also to Cara and Jax for your guidance and collective wisdom, expertise and generosity throughout the editorial process.

We are thrilled by this opportunity to work with Harriet McInerney, Sophia Oravecz, Helen Koehne and the rest of the NewSouth Publishing team, and are grateful to Regine Abos for the beautiful cover design, and the original support of Brow Books for the book's first edition.

Both editions of *The Relationship is the Project* were assisted by the Australian Government through Creative Australia, its principal arts investment and advisory body. The first edition also received support from the Victorian Government through Creative Victoria and the Sidney Myer Fund through its Creative Fellowship initiative.

To all of the people who have read, reviewed or added *The Relationship is the Project* to curriculums and reading lists, invited us to curate or attend events, and helped raise the level of conversation about community-engaged practice in this country and beyond, as well as all of the artists, practitioners and communities we continue to work alongside: thank you.

This book is for you.
With love,
Jade Lillie and Kate Larsen